Real Food

A SPIRITUALITY
OF THE EUCHARIST

Robert Fabing, S.J.

PAULIST PRESS
New York/Mahwah

Imprimi Potest:
Paul Belcher, S.J.
Provincial
California Province of the Society of Jesus
January 5, 1993

Library of Congress Cataloging-in-Publication Data

Fabing, Robert, 1942-
     Real food: a spirituality of the Eucharist/Robert Fabing.
        p.   cm.
     Includes bibliographical references.
     ISBN 0-8091-3435-7 (pbk.)
     1. Lord's Supper—Catholic Church. 2. God—Love. 3. Spiritual life—Catholic Church. 4. Catholic Church—Doctrines. 5. Catholic Church—Liturgy. I. Title.
BX2230.2.F33   1993
234'.163—dc20   93-26902
                                                                                                        CIP

Published by Paulist Press
997 Macarthur Blvd.
Mahwah, N.J. 07430

Printed and bound in the
United States of America

Contents

IN LOVING MEMORY
OF MY FATHER,
JOSEPH PETER FABING

With Our Eyes Open

My first book, *The Eucharist of Jesus,* was essentially about the grace of the liturgy of the word and the eucharistic prayer in the eucharistic liturgy. This book, *Real Food,* centers its attention on the grace of the communion rite within the eucharistic liturgy. Its focus is the breaking of the bread and the distribution of the body and blood of Christ. For me it is a completion of the eucharistic dynamic.

The central theme of this book comes from the fact that the grace of the sacraments is given through the mode of action, the actions of all those participating in the sacrament. When we specify this in terms of the eucharist, the grace of the sacrament is ministered by Christ to us through the actions of all those present at the eucharistic liturgy. We receive the gifts of grace in a sacrament not with eyes closed, as private prayer would often have it, but with our eyes open. We receive the gifts of grace of a sacrament with our eyes open...not closed.

When we proceed up the communion aisle to receive the body and blood of Christ with our eyes open, we easily observe others in the same line. A common enough experience in such circumstances is to observe someone in the community we know who has serious problems, deficiencies, and is an obvious sinner in the public sense. Our instinctive reaction is, "Oh, I know that person. I know what that person has done. Why is that person here? How is that person in this line going up to communion?" But that person is! And the Lord Jesus is giving his body and blood over to this person as well as to ourselves. This can be a shock—especially to us who have equated prudent judgment, blameless behavior, and loyal simplicity with success in approaching the incomprehensible mystery of our God. If we keep our eyes open, however, and don't drop our head quickly down, we can observe our incomprehensible God. We can see what our God is doing in this sacrament, this eucharistic meal, this banquet of Jesus Christ. We can see whom Jesus invites to his table, whom Jesus wishes to be around him, and whom Jesus wishes to feed. We can see what our God is really like, and how our God acts. We can see who our God really is.

With our eyes open as we proceed up the communion line we can come to know our God. With our eyes open we can see what our God is doing. With our eyes open we can come to observe our God loving. The eucharistic love of Jesus is given out freely to everyone without charge. Jesus loves differently than we do. It is this divine love that we hunger and thirst to love with. We are fed by watching Jesus love.

As we experience the truth of this realization, the eucharist of the Lord becomes an ever deeper living home for us. Here is where we can come to be refreshed and filled with the very richness we have always wanted. Here we can come and see the people of God formed by the love of Christ. Here we can come and observe Christ's objective. We can feel Christ's changing action and love. This is where we are fed in a way that gives meaning and fulfillment to our lives.

It is this eucharistic love of Christ that is real food—the subject of this book. It is some of this experience that I wish to share with you, the reader.

The style of *Real Food* is different from the style of *The Eucharist of Jesus* not by design or by intent, but quite naturally and spontaneously. The very action of Jesus in the communion rite of the eucharist seems to inform, instruct, and create the change.

This book was a joy to write and, initially, just begins to express the riches of the real food of the eucharistic love of God given in and by Jesus. It is a gift that can only really be fully enjoyed in the experience of sitting down with Jesus at the eucharistic table.

I would like to thank Richard Draper, S.J., Walter Farrell,

S.J., Lucy Malarkey, S.H.C.J., and Dennis Smolarski, S.J. for their comments and reflections on reading this manuscript.

I have attempted in this book to use inclusive language as much as possible while, at the same time, doing no harm to the flow of the English language. I have referred to the first person of the Trinity as "Father" because of the biblical roots in Jesus and centuries-old Christian usage. I view God, however, as encompassing all of the richness of both male and female.

Robert Fabing, S.J.
Los Altos, California

Chapter One

Fast Food

Most men and women who are professional marriage counselors and family therapists are finding that no matter whom they see, husband or wife, they are saying the same thing over and over: Work doesn't work! Work is not enough! These health professionals find themselves counseling men and women who work twelve, thirteen, fourteen hours a day five and six days a week. These Catholic health professionals find themselves saying to career men and women that if you give ninety percent of your human energy, your intimate energy, to work and to the company, you are in trouble. They find themselves saying that it is immoral for a husband or a wife to come home in the evening having given ninety percent of his or her personal, intimate, emotional and human energy to work and to the company. They find themselves saying that human beings are not made for work; work is made for human beings.

Love and Work

They reflect with these husbands and wives on something that Sigmund Freud said (I am not a Freudian, but I do subscribe to this): "There are two problems that a human being must solve to be happy: the problem of love and the problem of work."

I believe in the last analysis, when all is said and done, at the end of our lives, whether we successfully or unsuccessfully have solved the issues of love in our lives and the issues of work, we will be able to say that each of these areas demanded some-

where around fifty percent of our human energy to solve successfully. We may not have resolved these needs during our lifetime
in a way that we could call successful or satisfying, but I think one
thing will be clear: love and work are equal exactors of dues.

The question then arises, "Do we spend fifty percent of our
intimate emotional energy, our human energy, on love and the
problems and issues around love? Do we spend fifty percent of
our intimate emotional and human energy, talent, and resources
on work? Or is our situation, as is the situation of most of the
people I see, that we spend ninety percent of our emotional and
intimate energy, time, talent, on work, the problems of the work
place, and the issues and needs of work? This leaves ten percent
of our human needs, our energy, our time, talent, and emotionality left over to spend on love, on the problems of love, and on
the issues, aspects, and dimensions of love.

90% Work—10% Love?

Most of the people these counselors are seeing in counseling are in the 90%–10% bracket. One could say, "Well, that's
why they are in counseling!" Their response to that observation
is certainly an affirmative, "Yes!" However, in many ways those
who seek out counseling are the lucky ones. Many of the people
seen on retreats for married couples have the same problem.
Many of the priests and sisters seen during the thirty-day, indi-
vidually directed, Spiritual Exercises of St. Ignatius Loyola have
the same problem. Most of these husbands and wives, priests,
and sisters are not in counseling and are not seeking counseling.
They all have the problem: 90% work–10% love.

It is pointed out to them that human beings are not made
for work, but that work is made for human beings. It is pointed
out to them that life is asking that they invest 50% of their
human energy and emotionality in the problems, demands,
needs, and issues of the work place and 50% of themselves, their
human and personal energy, in the problems, demands, needs,
and issues of love. It is pointed out that the source of their irri-

tability and impatience occurs when the problems, demands, needs, and issues of love begin to show themselves impinging on the 10% of human intimate energy they have "allotted" for the enterprise of love. They get "upset." They feel "put upon." They feel "victimized." They feel "a loss of freedom" and become irritable, impatient, angry, and simply resist. One feels that there is something very wrong here. One feels that life is wrong to be asking this, that the person or situation asking this is somehow out of line. One feels that this is "unjust" and that the claim being made on oneself by another is an intrusion into one's private time and energy. To live in any other life stance than 90% work–10% love is unrealistic and not a response to life that is practical. Their counselors' response to this is that it is immoral to live in this manner.

In the traditional family example, it is immoral for a man to come home with only 10% of his human energy for spouse and family, having given 90% of his energy to the company. It is immoral for a woman to have given 90% of her emotional and human energy to the children and be exhausted, drained, and have only 10% of her energy for her husband when he comes through the door in the evening. It is immoral for a career woman to spend 90% of her personal and human energy at work and come home to her husband and children with only 10% of her self energy to share. It is immoral for a priest or a sister to come to the evening meal with his or her community an exhausted wreck, having spent 90% of his or her energy working all day.

It is obvious that a great deal of counseling practice has come down to dealing with men and women who are devoting more time to work than they are to love. The result is a problem in the area of love.

What Does a Meal Mean Today?

Here is where the theme of this chapter comes into play. We begin this consideration with the question, "What does a meal mean today?" We could answer, "Good food, a nice cuisine, an intimate decor, a relaxed environment." Many would respond, "A microwaved frozen TV dinner before the television set." What you would not hear as often is, "Good company, good companionship, and good conversation." It is interesting to note here that the word "company" or "companionship" comes from the Latin words *cum* which means "with" and *pan* which means "bread." The word "company" or "companionship" means "sharing bread with someone" or "one with whom one eats."

The word "conversation" comes to us from the Latin word *conversari* through Middle French and Middle English. It means, as Webster puts it, "to live with, to share one's feelings with another, to share one's ideas with another and to have familiarity with another." The word "conversation" means to share affection, tenderness, emotion, and passion with another. The word "conversation" means to share one's beliefs, attitudes, convictions, perceptions, memories, dispositions, inclinations, mind set, propensities, and notions with another person. "Conversation" means to share one's intuition, motivation, and personhood, one's self verbally, with another. Conversation is the sharing of the truth of who one is with another. It is telling the story of who you are to another.

Companionship and Conversation

I am saying that there is a relationship between "companionship" and "conversation." I am saying that a meal means eating with another, breaking bread with another and sharing the truth of who one is with another. A meal is companionship and conversation. I think these two notions of sharing bread with another and sharing who you are with another are the very meanings of a meal. A meal is an experience not only of biological food but also of emotional, psychological, intellectual, and spiritual food: sustenance. "Human beings do not live by bread alone" (Matthew 4:4), says the Lord. And as Genesis states, "It is not good for human beings to be alone." What this is pointing up is that a meal for a human being is a social event. A meal is an event for the soul of a person as well as for the body. The complex hungers and needs we have come into play here. We have needs for physical food. We need meat, cheese, fish, chicken, potatoes, rice, pasta, bread, vegetables, water, milk, fruit, watermelon, apples, peaches, apricots, pears, desserts, chocolate, ice cream, cake, cookies, breakfast breads, coffee, tea, and on and on. We have needs for biological, physical sustenance and stimulation for energy to live. We also have emotional needs for personal sustenance, nourishment and for the emotional energy to live. We also have intellectual needs for sustenance and nourishment that require stimulation for us to live. We have love and friendship needs for sustenance and nourishment in order for us to be healthy.

Fast Food

We are complex beings, multi-dimensional with many levels. It takes a multiplicity of experiences, events, circumstances, and people to render us happy and satisfied and content. A meal is a human event that meets many of these needs. Obviously, the point here is that the social dimensions of a meal are important, very important. It can be said, and, I believe, successfully defended, that the social dimensions of a meal are even more important than the physical-biological ones. Today, with our workaholic tendencies, people eat and run. Or, better yet, we eat on the run. "Fast food" is a major American industry, and, through us, a major global industry. Its popularity is well established. Fast food means just what it says. You can get it fast. You don't have to wait for your meal. You can eat it fast. You can leave fast. In so many ways this concept has formed and shaped the notion of a meal in our culture. Fast food has come to mean fast meal. Phenomena such as the TV dinner have arisen that have been taken to heart by many in our culture. The TV dinner combines the need for fast food along with the need for company. There is someone to break bread with, and someone to have a conversation with, someone to share with: the TV.

Many in our culture eat their main meal in front of the television set. They meet their need for physical-biological food with a TV frozen dinner, and they meet their need for social contact with a television program.

This is the image of meal that many in our culture deal with. You ask people in our contemporary society what their image of "meal" is, what their experience of "meal" is, and their response is often one that resembles the following image. We see someone grabbing a cup of coffee running out the door with a commuter mug that keeps the coffee hot in the car on the freeway to work. We see a donut in a paper napkin that gets special attention when the bumper-to-bumper traffic grinds to a complete halt and one can balance the donut with one hand on the wheel of the car after putting the commuter mug of coffee down. All of this takes place as one's social needs for company and conversation are met by listening to the morning world and local news plus the helicopter traffic report on the car radio.

Let's Take a Lunch Break

One's image of lunch often is the fast food experience I have spoken of. It is appropriate to mention here that, as we all know, fast food is doing a flourishing business in this society and culture of ours in breakfast, lunch, and dinner hours. Lunch, however, can often be an experience of "picking up the loose ends of the morning meeting." The "lunch break syndrome" is what I have come to call it. This phenomenon is a very common experience where what is being worked upon in the meeting from 11:00 a.m. to 12 noon gets interrupted by someone saying, "Let's take a lunch break!" Everybody responds, "Great!" Everyone gets up and starts down the hall, enters the elevator, and then heads out to the nearest restaurant. Everyone sits down and orders lunch without missing a beat in the discussion about the material of the meeting. This becomes the "working lunch" where the prime topic of conversation is the material of the 11:00 a.m. to 12 noon meeting. What really is going on here is that this is actually a "meeting" with some physical-biological food provided to sustain one's biological needs enough to keep the matter at hand flowing. It is more work.

The adult business work place is not the only arena in our society in which this phenomenon takes place. Without going into many examples, simply reflect on school life. The phenomenon of the "lunch meeting" is one example. How many lunch meetings are there? The dance committee, the school newspaper, the drama club, the basketball team, the cheerleaders, have their organizational meetings during lunch where everyone sits at school desks with their brown bag lunch spread across the desk top as someone outlines the goals of the organization on the blackboard or offers a flow sheet calling upon everyone in the organization to agree, disagree, or give input. All of this activity of working on the organization is done during lunch because lunch is "the best time to nab everyone and have most people present." So it really is a meeting with some food there somewhere to attract as many members as possible. This is the image many have of the meaning of lunch and lunchtime.

The TV Dinner

The TV dinner image can be one of many dinner images that come to mind. In any event these images present themselves to us enough to recognize them as a part of us and as a part of our culture today. To say the least, these images present a problem. The meaning of "meal" and "mealtime" in our society today is in trouble.

We Don't Have Time for a Meal

To use the image of a meal as a value is a problem to us. To use the image of a meal as something that is of central value and importance brings the response, "What? Are you serious? We don't have time for a meal! You're talking about a sit-down dinner, and that is not practical in this day and age. This is a special event and not the norm in our culture."

So, really, one is dead in the water if one makes one's central image "a meal" because it really is somewhat of a meaningless experience in our contemporary society. The referent—that which the image images or refers to—isn't strong, isn't valued, or isn't experienced as important in our society. I say, "Agreed! The point is well made." Although I agree that this is the way it is in our society, I need to state that I view this "meaninglessness of a meal in our society" as a serious problem that needs to be addressed. This issue needs attention. It does not need to be shelved and dropped to the end of the agenda list as a luxury that is "fine to get to if you have the time."

Aching for True Loving Intimacy

I believe that this is a central symptom of a culture that is aching for true loving intimacy and simply does not know how to get it, nourish it, accept it, enjoy it, and share it. Considering that a meal is a central element of human life, I'd say we have a major problem here. Considering that love of one's neighbor and love of God are the two central commands of Jesus to us, I'd say we are settling ourselves at the heart of the problem as we get in a position to look at this matter. Because "a meal" is considered by our society and culture to be such an unimportant human event in terms of time, energy, effort and concern this does not make this consideration right. Because our technological culture manipulates the human experience of a meal to serve the god and goddess "work," this does not make doing this right. Because this is what we do does not make what we do right or good or valuable. On the contrary, what we are doing is not right, not good, not healthy, and not of real lasting human value. I cite the wreckage of human relationships in our culture and society as my evidence. I cite the over 60% divorce rate in our culture and society as evidence that there is a serious problem in our pursuit, attainment, acceptance, nourishment, enjoyment, and sharing of human love and intimacy.

The Meaninglessness of a Meal

I think the meaninglessness of mealtime is a central symptom of this lack of knowledge of what it means to be human and to remain fruitfully human. Do we have the need for company and conversation? The answer is a deep and resounding "Yes!" Are we as a society meeting that need? I would suggest "No!" Are we taking the time and making the effort to meet our own needs for intimacy? I would say on a broad cultural basis, "No!" Do we know how to do this? I would say, "No!" Are we willing to look at ourselves and our lives and adjust to our own needs in a way that resolves them? I would say, "Not very well!" So we have a problem. I would like to begin this work on sharing a meal with the recognition of this problem and continue as a means of resolving it to point out a possible solution by exposing the riches of the meal the Lord Jesus invites us to.

As part of an introduction to this, let us look at examples of this meal experience from two other cultures.

If you have been involved with other cultures or lived in foreign countries you may have had another experience of eating a meal. Americans who have been to Italy often smile as stories are shared about the Italian daily schedule. The smile is a sort of "sub rosa" way of expressing our notion of "how impractical" a schedule it is to design one's entire day around eating the main meal which takes place in the middle of the day. Those who have experienced Italy know that the Italians have their largest meal at noon. Most work stops in Italy at noontime. Families gather together at this time, and they spend an hour to an hour and one half eating and sharing at table. After this noon meal they retire for an hour siesta.

The main meal in the Italian culture seems to absorb a great deal of attention insofar as it is mentioned so often as a point of reference throughout the day. One starts work at 8:00

am and is continually relating one's work project over against the time of finishing up by 12:30 pm so as to be able to get to one's main meal. In Italy it is not generally an accepted mode of living to work through 12:30 pm to 3:00 pm in the afternoon. Most work activity stops as one gathers together with one's loved ones around the family table.

Anyone who has spent time in the Arab world also has experienced a similar phenomenon. Arab cuisine is dominated by what they refer to as mezza. Mezza is the Arab equivalent to the Italian preparation before the main entree: soup, salad, hors d'oeuvres, antipasto, and pasta. Mezza is the Arab preparation for the main entree of the meal. Mezza is different, however, not in quantity, but in that it reflects the Arab environment: hot desert surroundings. Most Arab culture is geographically situated in hot arid desert environs. This occasions the need to cool down at mealtime. Mezza, then, is a combination of cool salads and dips that can be put in pita or pocket bread. It is common that mezza consists of fifteen to twenty different types of salads and dips. This is all before the main entree. I describe all of this not to make us all salivate, as I'm sure it does, but to bring to light what the Arab culture offers for the main meal. It is a lot of food. When one first experiences an Arab main meal, one is overwhelmed by the variety of food presented. From the simple standpoint of time, one is required by the cuisine itself to remain and invest one's physical presence. It's hard to face a table of fifteen to twenty salads and dips served with pocket bread and take it all in physically in ten to fifteen minutes. One needs more time.

An Excuse To Talk and Spend Time Together

What is on the table demands that one stay there for at least a full hour. This is the Arab culture. Don't misunderstand me or the Arab culture here. The idea is not to overeat. The idea that the Arab culture is offering and presenting is "to stay a long time at table." The variety of what is presented allows one to pick and choose what one physically eats. This, of course, is used as an excuse to talk, share, and spend time with one's family, friends, and guests. The evening main meal in the Arab culture is indeed a main event. It is a big deal. It can easily take two hours. Is overeating the agenda? No! Spending time together is the agenda, and the variety of flavors presented is the insurance that this will take place. The physical food is an excuse and way to gather people together and be with one another. Isn't this the whole idea of a meal?

Food Is a Social Event

A meal is a social event. It is a human experience that nourishes our human needs for intimacy, emotionally and psychologically, as well as nourishing our physical bodies with food. "Human beings do not live by bread alone" (Matthew 4:4).

If you ask yourself, "Whom do people ask to go on vacation with them? Whom do people want to spend their vacation with? Whom do I want to spend my vacation with?" the answer comes readily back, "Friends! My friends!" I think this is an experience that is easy enough to identify with. When we think of taking a week or two off for our yearly vacation we think of doing it with our friends, and, basically, with our friends only. Why? Well, if you are like me, our one or two week vacation a year is a very precious time. It is a very special time. For one thing it is special because it is one or two weeks out of fifty-two. It is also special and precious because it is a time for us to "let our hair down" and "be ourselves" in a very different environment. It is this element and need for "letting our hair down" and "being ourselves" that calls out our true selves. This is what we want to be: "our true selves." This need demands the presence of our true friends. So when we go on vacation we want our true friends to be with us. This brings us joy and love and lifts our spirits.

A Mini Vacation

A meal is meant to be a "mini vacation." A meal is meant to be seen and understood and experienced as a "mini-time to let your hair down and be your true self." A meal is meant to be an event that gives us the human experience of being our true selves in joy. A meal is meant to re-create us.

A meal is meant to be taken with friends, and the nourishment is meant to be more than physical. It is meant to be the food of human intimacy, and the result is to be love and joy.

As we look back over the examples found in Italian society and in Arabic culture we find a definite meeting of this human need for physical-biological nourishment, the human need for intimacy, both emotionally and psychologically, and also our human intellectual and spiritual needs. "Human beings are not meant to live on bread alone" (Matthew 4:4).

These meal scenes from various cultures around the world are the events of their daily human lives together. They are valued experiences and valued human events. It is this experience of a "meal together" that I would like to focus on because it is on this experience that Jesus shared and focused the meaning of his life and his reign: the heavenly banquet.

QUESTIONS FOR PERSONAL AND COMMUNITY REFLECTION AND DISCUSSION

1. What was your experience of a meal today?

2. What was breakfast like for you today? Lunch? And especially your main dinner meal?

3. Share this experience in your group.

4. What was the experience of other group members?

5. Recall your experiences of breakfast, lunch, and your main dinner meal as you were growing up.

6. Share this in your groups.

7. What effect did these experiences have on you? on forming who you are?
   a. What are you pleased with?
   b. What was painful?
   c. What could you have changed?
   d. What happened that you are glad about?

8. Share these experiences in your prayer with God.

9. Share these experiences in your group.

Chapter Two

The Wedding Feast at Cana

As we begin to look at Jesus, I would like to suggest a way of experiencing him in these following chapters. The way or method that I would like to present in each of these meal experiences of Jesus is essentially that used and developed by St. Ignatius Loyola, the founder of the Society of Jesus, the Jesuits, in his Spiritual Exercises. Ignatius calls this way, this method of prayer, "contemplation." The four sections within the Spiritual Exercises of St. Ignatius are each referred to as a "week." The first week lends itself to the method of prayer Ignatius would call "meditation." The second, third, and fourth weeks are the subject of the method of prayer Ignatius would call "contemplation." Without going into an exhaustive consideration of this subject let it suffice here to say that meditation for Ignatius implies the primary usage of one's intellect. One asks questions of oneself and considers the realities of evil in the world and in one's life. For Ignatius, as the subject of the "week" changes, the method of prayer changes.

This change follows a well-defined epistemological principle. The study of how a human being comes to know something is called epistemology. It is based on the principle that the method you use to know something is determined and formed by what you are coming to know. If I want to get to know the multiplication tables I memorize them. After I do that I can say that I know the multiplication tables. If I want to get to know a person I have to change my method. If I want to get to know a person and I say, "I'll memorize that person," it doesn't work. The method of memorization works with multiplication tables, but somehow it does not work with a human person. You need another method. You need another way to come to know a human being. You can't memorize a person. It doesn't work. If you want to get to know a person you have to be with that person. You must be with people as they relax and have fun, as they recreate, as they socialize, as they share a meal, and as they work. One needs to be with people to find out what they like to read, what kind of movies they like and don't like, what kind of food they like or don't like, what they like to do, how they react at work or at home. It takes a long time of being with a person through many varied experiences to come to know that person.

It is the same in the Spiritual Exercises of St. Ignatius. After the first week of the Exercises, the life and actions of Jesus of Nazareth are the subject matter for one's prayer. The person of Jesus is the center of one's prayer. Ignatius has us ask for an intimate knowledge of the Lord as a person and an intimate love of the Lord as a person. How does one do this? By "being with" the Lord Jesus. How can one "be with" Jesus in a way that results in an intimate and familiar knowledge and love of Christ?

The Prayer of Contemplation

Ignatius offers the method of contemplation. This method of prayer calls us to use our imagination. The method Ignatius proposes is given in five steps. The first is the making of an act of the presence of God. The second is to read the episode in the life of Christ you wish to contemplate. The third is for us to ask God for the grace one wishes—an intimate knowledge of the Lord as a person and an intimate love of the Lord as a person. The fourth is to contemplate the gospel scene of the life of Jesus that you have selected. This is the body of one's prayer period occupying most of one's prayer time. The fifth, and final, step is to thank God for what has transpired in your prayer.

The first three of these steps should take no more than one minute each. I would like to point out that making an act of the presence of God is not stopping and seeing God. No. An act of the presence of God is stopping for a moment as I begin prayer and realizing not that I see God but that God sees me. This act of the presence of God is bringing into my consciousness that God is aware of me, that God knows me, that God knows everything that is in my heart, and that I am in God's presence. This act of the presence of God is meant to issue in a sense that Psalm 139 expresses, "Yahweh, you know me. You know if I am standing or sitting."

The second step is a brief reading of the text that I have selected. This reading is meant to be done at a comfortable, relaxed, prayerful pace.

The third step is to pray for what I desire. Here I will pray for an intimate knowledge of the Lord as a person and an intimate love of the Lord as a person.

The fourth step is the major portion of this prayer. Ignatius gives the method of "being with" a person in order to achieve this sense of familiarity and loving friendship. The method he puts forth is one that involves the use of our imagination. Ignatius suggests that with the eye of our imagination we see the scene that we wish to contemplate, to pray on. With our imagination we see all of the individuals in the episode we choose to contemplate. In this experience of Jesus we would see Jesus, his apostles, and countrymen, women, and children. Ignatius asks us to proceed with our imagination to hear the words of Jesus as he speaks to the people. We are invited to feel the heat of the sun, taste the dust, and then touch Jesus, the other apostles, the members of the crowd, or whomever we are moved to converse with.

The Effect of Contemplation

Here the prayer of contemplation begins to have its effect. As we center ourselves in the scene from scripture becoming exactly as we are today, we share with those in the scene whatever we would wish. We speak with whomever we are moved to speak with. We touch whomever we wish to touch. We say exactly what is on our minds or in our hearts as our prayer develops. We are simply ourselves, asking for what we wish, praying for what we need, loving as we would love. The gift of contemplation in the Ignatian sense is that we talk to Jesus as a friend. We listen to Jesus as a friend. We receive the gift of intimate knowledge of the Lord as a person and intimate love of the Lord as a person: intimate friendship. This is prayer. This is the method we use to get to know and love a person: be with that person.

I suggest you use this method of prayer on the meal experiences of Jesus that we are looking at in this work as well as the entire life of Jesus presented to us by the gospel writers.

The Person of Jesus

We now begin to look at and contemplate the person of Jesus. I have been struck by how often in the gospels Jesus dines with people. These meal experiences of Jesus are the subject of this consideration. It is an apt point of interest because Jesus himself has called us all to his heavenly banquet: eternal life.

The Experience of a Meal for Jesus

What was the experience of a meal for Jesus in his culture and his times? I think this is a valid and legitimate question given the cultural analyses we have just been through in the first two chapters. I would like to proceed in an investigation of this question by means of a brief consideration of the early Hebrew experience of a meal, and then proceed to a description of what a normal meal would have been like during the time of Christ. I think this will help in developing an understanding of why Jesus chose the image of a meal as central to him, to who he was, and to what his kingdom and rule is all about.

In the period which we have come to speak of as biblical times, from circa 2000 B.C. to about 100 A.D., it was the custom of semitic peoples to have two meals a day. They would have one meal in the morning and one in the evening. The normal eating experience in a home during the times of the Old and New Testaments was one where the meal was served on a mat that was laid out upon the floor. Those who were eating would lie down on the mat and lean backward, usually resting on their elbow. This left their other hand and arm available to reach for food. All of the food was taken and eaten by hand since the knife, fork, and spoon had not made their appearance as yet. If you have the possibility of dining at an Ethiopian restaurant in your area or even a Moroccan restaurant, you have a very good chance of experiencing what this style of eating would have been like. From the archaeological evidence we have now of Old and New Testament cuisine, it appears that there were many dishes. The number and variety of extant pottery from the times and locale point to this.

Customs surrounding a meal seem to have been dictated by the Pharisees within Judaism. The custom was that you must wash before eating. If you came in from outside the home, you had to wash your feet. There was a kiss of greeting and an anointing of the head of a guest. At formal dinners guests were even expected to wear a festive garment which was usually white. Usually, the host would serve some specially prepared small dish to the guests.

In Egypt and Mesopotamia, tables and reclining couches were customary, but these were only for royalty and for the very wealthy. The Ashurbanipal reliefs that have been preserved in the British Museum show this. It seems that the very wealthy in Israel did adopt this type of furniture for their meals. This developed through Greek and Roman influences during New Testament times to a table that was semicircular, a kind of horseshoe shape, that was very low to the ground. This type of table would allow those who were eating the meal to reach their food from a reclining position on couches around the table. The individuals would then lean on their elbows and serve themselves with their free hand.

> ## Food for Our Imagination

With this background let us begin our scriptural consideration.

Three days later there was a wedding feast at Cana in Galilee. The mother of Jesus was there, and Jesus and his disciples had also been invited. When they ran out of wine, since the wine provided for the wedding was all finished, the mother of Jesus said to him, "They have no wine." Jesus said, "Woman, why turn to me? My hour has not come yet." His mother said to the servants, "Do whatever he tells you." There were six stone water jars standing there that were for the ablutions that are customary among the Jews: each could hold twenty or thirty gallons. Jesus said to the servants, "Fill the jars with water," and they filled them to the brim. "Draw some out now," he told them, "and take it to the steward." They did this; the steward tasted the water, and it had turned into wine. Having no idea where it came from—only the servants who had drawn the water knew—the steward called the bridegroom and said, "People generally serve the best wine first, and keep the cheaper sort till the guests have had plenty to drink; but you have kept the best wine till now." This was given at Cana in Galilee. He let his glory be seen and his disciples believed in him.

John 2. 1-11

I would like to begin a consideration of this event in the life of Jesus with an elementary description of the scene. My being a Jesuit is showing, I know. However, I believe, as St. Ignatius in his method of contemplation would suggest, that setting the scene with food for our imagination is helpful. Present-day Cana is a very small village located some five miles northeast of Nazareth. It is on a gentle slope extending downward and eastward toward a fertile plain. The village looks out eastward toward the Sea of Galilee, but the lake does not come into view because it is some six hundred feet below sea level and some ten miles away. It is through Cana that Jesus walked as he journeyed from Nazareth to Capernaum, which is on the Sea of

Galilee. The distance of the journey would have been some twenty miles.

Since archaeologists have estimated that Nazareth at the time of Christ was a town of about one hundred and twenty-five people, it is reasonable for us to assume from contemporary studies that Cana was no larger. Even present-day Cana is not much larger. The soil is rocky but gardens abide which have been carefully cleared of stones. This is not the case of the rich fertile soil of the plain extending northeastward from the foot of the Cana slope. Cana and its surrounding undulating hills are covered with low lying green grass in the spring and dry grass in the summer and fall. Cana is in a lush area of Israel. It is interesting to note that there is a difficulty that a writer such as myself who has visited Cana many times and studied the area for many years has. The difficulty is that there really is not much to say about Cana. It is a very small town with a very small-town, unspectacular history.

This situates for us in a very interesting way the comments of Nathanael who was from Cana. As John has it Philip found Nathanael "under the fig tree" and told him of Jesus saying,

> "We have found the one Moses wrote about in the law, the one about whom the prophet wrote: He is Jesus son of Joseph from Nazareth." Nathanael responded to Philip, "From Nazareth? Can anything good come from that place?"
>
> John 1: 43-45

If this is the comment about Nazareth from a resident of Cana at the time of Christ (and Cana is such an insignificant and small unnoticed village), how insignificant and small and unnoticed must Nazareth have been? The answer seems obvious.

In any event, the proximity of Cana to Nazareth is not only physical in terms of distance but also the similarity extends in terms of the number of inhabitants and the nature of the village. It was small and "small town" in nature. It was a country village. A wedding there was a country wedding. Guests would have been country people. The guests were men who worked with their hands, women who were mothers and housewives. The guests were men who were farmers and herders, women who made their own clothes, men who built their own homes, women who baked their own bread, and children of the fields. It is not too hard to imagine that the bride and groom may have been relatives of Jesus. Certainly the relationship had a family dimension in that both Jesus and his mother Mary were invited.

Since both Jesus and Mary were invited, it is reasonable for us to assume that the couple who were getting married or their families knew both Jesus and Mary. They may have known Jesus or Mary separately; however, if this were so, then they knew that if they invited and wanted one of them to come it would be courteous and, really, the loving thing to do to invite them both. However it happened, Jesus and Mary find themselves present at this country wedding.

A Country Wedding Feast: Who Was There?

The story is familiar to us. We know of the Jewish customs at weddings, and the gospel account directly states that the wine ran out. This implicitly points to a meal that Jesus partook of during this wedding celebration. It was a wedding feast, a country wedding meal. This is the first account we have of Jesus eating with anyone in the gospels. We can assume that the style of the meal, the cuisine, the time involved, the furnishings, and the environment were probably very much like what was described in the beginning of this chapter. What I would like to focus on is whom Jesus sat down to table with. Whom did Jesus eat with? Whom did Jesus share a meal with?

The first episode in the public life of Jesus, as we have it in the gospels, where he shared a meal with anyone was here. Jesus shared a meal with people from Cana in Galilee. This is an astounding fact when you stop to think about it. People from Cana in Galilee! Today, if you look at popular guide books of Israel, Cana does not even appear, not even in the indices in the back of the books! If the insignificance of Cana is so today, what must it have been like at the time of Christ? Christ shared a meal with the people of Cana. The people of Cana were insignificant people. Cana was an unimportant village. Cana remains marginal today. It was doubly borderline in the time of Christ. There is simply nothing really to be found about the town in history. No one of great importance ever came from there. No one who ever contributed greatly to the history of the world ever came from there. There was really nothing written about Cana at the time of Christ which is not all that different from today.

Cana found favor with God, however. So let the facts of history speak for themselves. Jesus shared his first meal of the gospels with the people of Cana. Jesus spent time there. Jesus sat down at table with the simple country folk of the village and shared bread and wine, companionship, and conversation. Jesus extended his companionship to them. Jesus "shared bread" with them. Jesus shared himself with them. Jesus "shared the truth of himself" with them, his viewpoints, his feelings, his convictions, and his very self. Jesus had conversation with them. He told the story of who he was with them. With whom did Jesus share this meal? With the nobodies of Cana and the surrounding environs, including Nazareth. Jesus shared himself with men who had very little money, with women who had very little schooling, with men whose occupation was plowing the fields their fathers plowed, with women who used the same recipes their mothers used, with men whose concern was to have enough food to eat for themselves and their families, with women whose concern was to keep a house clean and have clean, clothed children.

These concerns are country people's concerns. These are simple and good people. They are so simple that the world has passed them and their town by as not being important or noticeable in any way for any reason. But Jesus did not think so. Jesus did not find them insignificant. Jesus did not find their town unnoticeable. Jesus did not find their concerns unimportant. Jesus found them very important and very noticeable. Jesus found them very significant. Jesus found them and their concerns very important—so much so that he shared his presence with them. He dined with them. He listened to them. He told them who he was. Jesus endeared Cana and the people of Cana to the whole world forever. Jesus put Cana and the people of Cana and the environs "on the map" of the hearts of generations forever by sharing a meal with them.

A Radically Different Viewpoint

Jesus begins his ministry by sharing a meal with these country "nobodies." There is a message for us in this as we contemplate this scene. Jesus loves these people. The love of God in Jesus is teaching us how we can become who we've always wanted to be because Jesus is "the way, the truth, and the life" (John 14·1) It is in Jesus that we will be who we've always wanted to be. We will be who we've always wanted to be only by looking into the eyes of Jesus, by watching him, and by keeping our eyes on him. As we watch Jesus share a meal with these country men, women, and children, we begin to see as God sees, to value as God values, to pay attention to what God pays attention to, and to love with the love of God. Jesus is showing us the nature of his reign here. At first blush it is plain to see. Jesus thinks plain and simple country peasants are significant, important, and deeply valuable. This unleashes a radically different viewpoint into human consciousness: the viewpoint of God. The Hebrew scriptures, the Old Testament, is full of direct and indirect references alluding to God's penchant to judge not by appearances but to judge by the heart of a person. God sees the heart. God knows the human heart. This is the real miracle here, and it occurred during a festival meal.

QUESTIONS FOR PERSONAL AND COMMUNITY REFLECTION AND DISCUSSION

1. Give yourself the time to explore the method of prayer: contemplation.

2.   Spend one minute making an act of the presence of God.

3.   Give yourself two or three minutes to peacefully read John 2:1-11, the wedding feast at Cana.

4.   Allow yourself to be in this gospel scene, feeling the heat of the sun, hearing the music, experiencing the dancing, smelling the wedding banquet foods, and seeing Jesus, Mary, and the apostles.

5.   Be yourself there as you are here and now as a person. Allow your reactions and responses.

6.   Express yourself to Jesus, Mary, and the apostles in any way you wish. Speak plainly and directly, as one friend to another. This is the prayer of Ignatian contemplation.

7.   Share your experience in your group.

Chapter Three

Dinner with Levi

This experience of Jesus with Levi is given us as the heart of the second chapter of the gospel of Mark. The context is the very beginning of the public ministry of Jesus, and the scene is the area around the Sea of Galilee. This encounter of Jesus with Levi is situated immediately following the story of the paralytic being lowered through the roof to Jesus. This event happened in Capernaum, which is located on the northern shore of the Sea of Galilee.

> He went out again on the shore of the lake; and all the people came to him and he taught them. As he was walking on he saw Levi the son of Alphaeus, sitting by the customs house, and he said to him, "Follow me." And he got up and followed him.
>
> Mark 2:13-14; Luke 5:27-28; Matthew 9.9

In his honor Levi held a great reception in his house, and with them at table was a large gathering of tax collectors and others. The Pharisees and their scribes complained to his disciples and said, "Why do you eat and drink with tax collectors and sinners?" Jesus said to them in reply, "It is not those who are well who need the doctor, but the sick. I have not come to call the virtuous, but sinners to repentance."

> Matthew 9:10-12; Mark 2:15-17; Luke 5:29-32

As Mark has it, "He went out again to the shore of the lake" (Mark 2:13). Capernaum lies on a level plain which

29

extends back from the Sea of Galilee, some five hundred yards
to low-lying, rolling hills which extend further north. Directly to
the east two to three miles is the sight of ancient Bethsaida
where Jesus cured the blind man in Mark 8:22. Bethsaida is
located in a low-lying delta area formed by the Jordan River's
meandering entrance into the lake. Capernaum, then, is on the
westward edge of this plain-like area. It is on solid ground,
however, and a natural site for a small fishing village which it
was at the time of Christ.

Some of the archaeological ruins at Capernaum are said to
be the house of St. Peter. There is nothing to disprove this or
contradict the assumption that this indeed is the site of the actual house of Peter. On the contrary, persistent veneration of this
sight in the pre-Constantinian era points to its validity. Jewish
persecution of this site also supports that generations of
Christians after the death of Jesus held this site as holy, as
Peter's house and town, and as Jesus' "own city" (Matthew 9:1).

More immediate to our consideration is the life situation of
Capernaum at the time Jesus himself lived there. After King
Herod died his kingdom was divided. Herod Antipas received
the area where Capernaum was located. His brother Philip
received the territory on the other side of the Jordan River to the
east. As Capernaum was the first town that travelers would
arrive at after leaving Philip's territory, Herod Antipas
equipped it with a customs office and a small garrison of soldiers under a centurion's command.

The Life Situation of Capernaum

The poor economic condition of the inhabitants of
Capernaum at the time is evident from Luke 7:1-10, as it was the
centurion, a Gentile, who had to build the Jews their own syna-
gogue. The scene as we have it here is one of a town of poor
Jewish peasant fishermen, their families, and a Roman office of
taxation.

The town of Capernaum extended some five hundred

yards along the shoreline of the lake. Jesus was instructing the people as he walked along the shoreline. As he walked along he came to the customs house and saw Levi sitting there. As scripture has it he said to Levi, "Follow me." And Levi got up immediately and followed him (Matthew 2:14).

The People Considered Levi Untrustworthy

Levi was a common Jewish name, after the founder of one of the twelve tribes of Israel. Levi was a Jew, and Levi held a Roman governmental position. Israel was a garrisoned country. The Jews accepted Roman rule because Roman soldiers were everywhere. Rome taxed the countries they occupied for their own purposes. Roman taxation was collected for them by local wealthy businessmen who paid a set fee for a contract to collect taxes in a given area. The tax collector, or publican, was assigned a quota of funds to collect in a given time period. If he failed to collect his allotted sum of money he had to pay it out of his own resources. Any money left over, however, was the tax collector's to keep. Given this system, abuse was rampant. In order to make a profit a tax collector had to demand more money than the actual percentage the government had levied. The ordinary person knew this, and the resentment of the people toward a tax collector was high. A tax collector was one who had sold out his integrity to the foreign occupying establishment. "Untrustworthy" is a kind way of expressing the sentiment of the ordinary person vis-à-vis a tax collector.

Levi was stationed at a Roman taxation branch office at Capernaum. The customs office there probably levied taxes on travelers entering or leaving the town. They collected the taxes on road tolls, harbor tolls, import and export duties, goods brought to markets, and trade and professional licenses. Levi was guilty in the eyes of his fellow Jews of not being patriotic and of conspiring to oppress his own. He was not liked.

A Devastating Challenge

As the gospel writer of Mark begins this account Jesus is walking along the lake shore teaching the crowds that are walking with him. He is about to teach those walking with him something devastatingly challenging. In full view and earshot of those who are hanging on every word that is coming from the mouth of Jesus, Jesus' eyes rest on the untrustworthy, despicable, less than a worm of a man, Levi, the tax collector. Jesus issues him the ultimate sign of his love. He says, "Follow me"— which means "Be with me. I want you to be in my inner circle of confidants. I want you to be a bearer of my name. I want you to image me, and I want others to say that you are one of mine." Intimacy! Intimate love and friendship!

Levi "got up and followed him" (Mark 2:14). The joy of Levi, the tax collector, must have been boundless, as Luke writes in 9:29:

> In Jesus' honor Levi held a great reception in his
> house, and with them at table was a large gathering
> of tax collectors and others.

What we have come to see from contemporary historical and sociological studies was that Levi was a wealthy man. He had the means to hold a "great reception," and probably he had the home to do the same. The significance of all of this is that Jesus was there. The event of importance is that Jesus accepted an invitation to come to a "great reception in his honor" in Levi's home. The event of importance is that Jesus sat down at table with Levi and his tax collector friends. Jesus shared a meal with untrustworthy and despised people in a home that was paid for through the means of unjust oppression and fraud. Jesus broke bread with these people. Jesus was "company" to them and they to Jesus. Jesus had "conversation" with them and they with Jesus. Jesus shared his thoughts and feelings, his desires, his vision, and his dreams with them. Jesus shared who he was with them, and they shared who they were with him. Jesus spent time with them. Jesus spent himself with them.

It is not difficult to picture in one's imagination this scene of Jesus at table with Levi and his tax collector friends. We see Jesus engaging them in conversation, listening to them, and enjoying the cuisine of the day. Jesus is allowing himself to be known by them. Jesus is allowing them to know that they have access to him. This probably astounded the tax collectors most of all.

His Interest Rendered Them Defenseless

These were men who had hardened themselves. Knowing full well that they would be rejected by their own people, they went ahead and became tax collectors. These men could take punishment. They were accustomed to it. They expected it. Jesus' sitting down in their midst, in their environment, on their terms, offering them bread, himself, his time, and his interest, must have rendered them defenseless.

This ease and invitation of accessibility which Jesus extends here changes the outlook of these hardened tax collectors. The resultant lack of need to defend oneself brings joy. Jesus is eating with tax collectors. As we can see the scene and hear the dinner conversation get a bit louder and freer as everyone relaxes, a sense of comfort and naturalness begins to emerge between Jesus and the tax collectors. As this occurs we hear the words of the scribes and Pharisees as they look upon the same scene, "Why does he eat with tax collectors and sinners?" The scribes and Pharisees are simply echoing the question of the Jews who were following Jesus along the lake listening to his teaching, "Why did he ask a tax collector to be one of his intimate followers?"

The question that the scribes and Pharisees ask has the kind of deeper significance that we have considered here. The question "Why does he eat with tax collectors and sinners?" has a deeper meaning. The question also means, "Why does Jesus associate with tax collectors? Why does Jesus talk to them? Why does Jesus share himself with them? Why does Jesus accept their invitation and allow them to gain access to him? Why does Jesus break bread with them? Why does he spend time with them and have conversation with them?"

All of these questions emerge here because this is what it means to eat with someone. This is what it means to share a meal with someone.

The scribes and Pharisees would not share a meal with tax collectors. They would not associate with them or spend time with them. The scribes and Pharisees would not share themselves with the tax collectors. They would not listen to them. They would not break bread with them.

Jesus does.

Jesus answers their question. Jesus tells them "why."

When Jesus heard this he said to them, "It is not the healthy who need the doctor, but the sick. Go and learn the meaning of the words: 'What I want is mercy, not sacrifice.' I did not come to call the virtuous, but sinners."

Matthew 9:12-13

Learning Who God Is

Jesus wants to be with the tax collectors. Jesus wants Levi to be with him. It is the desire of Jesus, the love of Jesus, that we see here. We are learning who Jesus is. We are learning who God is. We are learning what the love of God is like. We are being taught here who God is. As the writer of John says, "God is love" (1 John 4:8).

The love of God has sought out the despicable, the untrustworthy, the lowest of the low. The love of God has made them the beloved ones. Jesus brought this meal on himself. He chose Levi. He allowed the whole event to unfold. Jesus wanted to share a meal with them.

I believe this says a great deal about God.

Our God is interested in mercy and compassion as Jesus charges the scribes and Pharisees: "Go and learn the meaning of the words: 'What I desire is mercy, not sacrifice'" (Matthew 9:13). It is understanding love and compassion that Jesus is giving in sharing a meal with Levi and his tax collector friends. It is seeking out the lost sheep. It is Jesus extending himself. It is Jesus desiring only goodness for the other. Jesus shares at the meal. Jesus wants to dine with them. Jesus loves them.

QUESTIONS FOR PERSONAL AND COMMUNITY REFLECTION AND DISCUSSION

1. Who are the "tax collectors" in your life?

2. What "buttons" in you do these people (or does this person) push?

3. What is this "button" in you all about? Where did it come from?

4. What are the experiences from your past history that go to make up these reactions? Who are the people in these memories?

5. Have these experiences been healed?

6. Allow yourself the time in prayer to bring these memories, the experience, and the people involved before Jesus.

7. Give thanks for the grace and your ability to do this.

8. Share this process in your group.

Chapter Four

The Feeding of the Five Thousand

Contemporary Tabgha is the place where "the feeding of the five thousand" is said to have occurred. Tabgha is a low-lying plain on the northern edge of the Sea of Galilee. The plain extends from the shoreline about three hundred yards to the base of a hillside. It is approximately one and a half miles west of Capernaum. It is here that contemporary veneration attributes the miracle of the feeding of the five thousand. The newly built church of the miracle incorporates the ancient Christian church mosaics of the loaves and fishes, continuing a strong Christian tradition of veneration of this site.

The gospel writers depict the experience:

Jesus went off to the other side to the Sea of Galilee—or of Tiberias—and a large crowd followed him, impressed by the signs he gave by curing the sick. Jesus climbed the hillside, and sat down there with his disciples. It was shortly before the Jewish feast of Passover.

Looking up, Jesus saw the crowds approaching and said to Philip, "Where can we buy some bread for these people to eat?" He only said this to test Philip; he himself knew exactly what he was going to do. Philip answered, "Two hundred denarii would only buy enough to give them a small piece each." One of his disciples, Andrew, Simon Peter's brother, said,

"There is a small boy here with five barley loaves and two fish; but what is that among so many?" Jesus said to them, "Make the people sit down." There was plenty of grass there, and as many as five thousand men sat down. Then Jesus took the five loaves and the two fish, raised his eyes to heaven, and said the blessing over them; then he broke them and handed them to his disciples to distribute among the crowd, giving out as many as they wanted. When they had eaten enough he said to his disciples, "Pick up the pieces left over, so that nothing gets wasted." So they picked them up, and filled twelve baskets with scraps left over from the meal of five barley loaves. The people, seeing this sign that he had given, said, "This is the prophet who is to come into the world."

John 6:1-14; Luke 9:16

As we begin our consideration of "the feeding of the five thousand," the plain and hillside of Tabgha on the northern shore of the Sea of Galilee can emerge in our imagination. Jesus, wanting to take his apostles away to a lovely place for some rest, is met by the people whom he was attempting to leave. He is moved with compassion at the sight of the crowd and teaches them of the reign of God and heals their sick. As late afternoon approaches, the disciples and Jesus engage in a conversation about how these people will be fed. Jesus solves the problem by taking the loaves and fishes present; "he raised his eyes to heaven, and said the blessing over them; then he broke them and handed them to his disciples to distribute among the crowd, giving out as much as they wanted" (Luke 9:16).

Here the image that we have to contemplate is the endless source of food being distributed from the arms of the apostles. On and on it goes until all present have as much as they want. On and on until all are filled! This indeed is a pre-figurement of the eucharistic bread and wine, the body and blood of Christ, endlessly passed out at the eucharistic liturgy down the years over the centuries in every country on earth. This is feeding the hungry and thirsty with eternal food.

Defenseless, Directionless, and Vulnerable

If we look closely at the five thousand, which the gospel writers say were actually many more, we see women and men and children who "were like sheep without a shepherd" (Mark 6:34). Jesus is moved with compassion for them and shares a meal with them. If we spend time with the image of "sheep without a shepherd," the first notion we come to is a sense that these people were helpless. Sheep are helpless without a shepherd. They are directionless. There is a sense of "no identity" about sheep when there is no shepherd. Sheep without a shepherd are pitiful and sad, like a lost child crying for its mother in a crowd of strangers. Sheep without a shepherd are defenseless. There is a great feeling of vulnerability, a sense of anxiety and fear at being open to being preyed upon. There is a kind of malaise inviting danger because they are expecting it.

Sheep without a shepherd appear in a very weak position. Sheep are very defenseless animals and are in vital need of the presence and guiding protection of a shepherd. Sheep are known to stand still as an attacking wolf devours them. The paralysis is one of fear that leads to death. Jesus uses this image for those with whom he shares a meal. Jesus shares a meal, his presence, and his conversation with them. Jesus breaks bread with and shares his company with those "who were like sheep without a shepherd": the weak. These are the ones whose weakness is showing: the defenseless, the needy, and those who are openly asking for their needs to be met. The weak are those who have no identity, those who are not sophisticated enough to hide their pain, those who are searching out of their ache and hunger. These are the vulnerable, the anxious, and the helpless.

It is these with whom the Lord shares himself here. It is these who the Lord says are his company. It is these to whom the Lord talks. It is these whom the Lord feeds. These are the ones whom the Lord takes care of and satisfies. These peasant hill country people who were following Jesus were beside themselves when they realized they were way out in a lonely place with nothing to eat. They had overstepped their bounds. They had let their hope and need get the better of them. They were in trouble. Once again they were vulnerable. Jesus gives them the gift of his compassionate loving food, satisfying them. He shared a meal with them. He spent time with them. He spent himself.

I quote the scripture here, since its power, given our interest, is a bit overwhelming.

Next day, the crowd that had stayed on the other side saw that only one boat had been there.... They crossed to Capernaum to look for Jesus. When they found him they said, "Rabbi, when did you come here?" Jesus answered:

"I tell you most solemnly,
you are not looking for me
because you have seen the signs
but because you had all the bread you wanted to eat.
Do not work for food that cannot last,
but work for food that endures to eternal life,
the kind of food the Son of Man is offering you
for on him the Father, God himself, has set his seal."

Then they said to him, "What must we do if we are to do the works that God wants?" Jesus gave them this answer, "This is working for God: you must believe in the one he has sent." So they said, "What work will you do? Our fathers had manna to eat in the desert; as scripture says: 'He gave them bread from heaven to eat.'" Jesus answered:

"I tell you most solemnly,
it was not Moses who gave you bread from heaven,

it is my Father who gives you the bread from heaven,
the true bread;
for the bread of God
is that which comes down from heaven
and gives life to the world."

"Sir," they said, "give us that bread always." Jesus
answered:

"I am the bread of life.
You who come to me will never be hungry."
                                             John 6:32-35

Jesus here begins an extensive commentary on his experience of feeding the five thousand. He does this through a con-
tinued dialogue with those he fed in sharing the meal. Those he
fed come looking for him again. When they find him Jesus says
to them, "You are not looking for me because you have seen the
signs but because you had all the bread you wanted to eat"
(John 6:26). Yes, Jesus explains himself, but the fact remains of
his initial words, "You are not looking for me." Jesus means this
here. What he is saying is that the crowd is not seeking the person of Jesus, who Jesus is, but they are seeking free food to fill
their stomachs. What disappointment Jesus must have experienced here. What rejection! Ultimately, I don't think Jesus or
you or I would have a problem with human beings seeking out
free food to fill their stomachs. After all, human beings are
human beings, and human beings have to eat. This is referred to
by the crowd as they quote their ancestors' need for daily bread
in the desert and God's sending them manna: "He gave them
bread from heaven to eat" (Exodus 16:4).

The Person of Jesus Was Unimportant

This is not the problem. The problem here is that this is
where the people stopped. They stopped at their stomach. Here

Jesus had shared a meal with them. He had shared himself with them. He had shared his person with them: who he was. He had chosen them as his company—he had broken bread with them. And he had had conversation with them. He had shared his feelings, his convictions, his thoughts, and his intimate desires with them. Jesus shared his own story with them. He had been himself with them. He had listened to them, and he had told them who he was. Their reaction to him as a person and to his sharing of who he was became a problem. Their reaction to his ability to listen and love them, to his choice to spend himself, his energy, and his time with them was a problem. It was a complex of imperviousness, disregard, neutrality, obliviousness, neglect, and a general sense that his personhood was unimportant. It was nonfunctional, non-valuable, and insignificant to them except for the fact that Jesus could supply free food for their physical bodies. Jesus erupts with an anger and a certain sadness and disappointment here. He says,

> Do not work for food that cannot last,
> but work for food that endures to eternal life,
> the kind of food the Son of Man is offering you,
> for on him the Father, God himself, has set his seal.
>
> John 6:27

Jesus reacts: "Do not work for," do not seek for, do not search for, do not put your energy into food that cannot last. Do not invest yourself and your time in food that cannot last "but work for"—seek for, search for, put energy into—"food that endures to eternal life."

Of course the crowd responds, "What are you talking about?" "What do you mean?" "What are the works that God wants?" Jesus responds, "This is working for God: you must believe in the one he has sent." Jesus is saying here that physical and biological food is not enough to sustain human life. "Human beings do not live by bread alone but on every word that comes from the mouth of God" (Matthew 4:4).

Working for God

The physical and biological food that the crowd seeks is only a small portion of the food Jesus has to offer to those that come to him. The kind of food that Jesus is offering is the food of his everlasting life. The crowd fixates on the word Jesus uses: "work." They ask about it. Jesus responds by modulating this fixation of the crowd on "work" into "belief in himself." Jesus attempts to move their attention into looking at him, his person, his selfhood, into listening to him, into loving him. "This is working for God." The crowd responds with what is in essence, "Why should we take our attentional energy away from our stomachs, our need for biological food, and become interested and invested in you as a person, Jesus of Nazareth?" "What sign will you give to show us that we should believe in you?" They then refer to Moses and their ancestors in the desert and to the manna from heaven. Manna was the daily bread left by Yahweh in the form of a hoar frost that settled on the leaves and ground around the wandering Hebrew people each morning. The people collected and harvested the manna each morning when they woke up and used it as flour for bread. Jesus identifies the provider by telling the people that it was not Moses who gave the bread, but it was his Father in heaven who gave the bread. Jesus says to them that his Father is now giving true bread, true food, from heaven that "gives life to the world." The people respond, "Give us this bread always." Jesus proclaims:

> I am the bread of life.
> You who come to me will never be hungry.
> You who believe in me will never thirst.
>
> John 6:35

"I am the food" is what Jesus is saying here. Jesus is crying out that what human beings hunger for is him, his love, his person. Jesus is saying that the deepest human hunger is for him, for love, for God. The deepest human hunger is for eternal life, to have fellowship with Jesus and to be in the company of Jesus.

The deepest human hunger is to have conversation with Jesus, to be heard by him, to be listened to by him and to listen to him. This hunger is to have communion with Jesus. This is eternal life. This is human activity that will last forever. This is human interaction that is eternal and everlasting.

This is human experience that goes to the roots of our being and that is open to transcendence. This is what it means to be open to forever living. This is food that will last. "Why spend your wages on what fails to satisfy?" (Isaiah 55).

You Missed It!

Jesus is reacting to all those who have their faces in their plates during meals. Jesus is reacting to those who have their attentional energy absorbed by reading the newspaper or those whose energy is fixated on the TV screen during meals. Jesus is saying, "You missed it! You missed being fed. You missed the real food of conversation and company." Jesus' message is, "You missed me," because "I am the bread of life. You who come to me will never be hungry. You who believe in me will never be thirsty." Jesus shares that to know him is eternal life and to know him is everlasting love. Jesus' message is that if you go to a meal and you miss the personal love of the individuals there at the table, you have missed the real food. You have not been fed. Jesus wants all to know that when you come to the meal the real food he shares is himself.

> Meanwhile the Jews were complaining to each other about him, because he had said, "I am the bread that came down from heaven." "We know his father and mother," they said.
>
> Jesus responded:
> "I tell you most solemnly,
> everybody who believes has eternal life.
> I am the bread of life.

Your fathers ate the manna in the desert
and they are dead;
but this is the bread that comes down from heaven
so that you may eat it and not die.
I am the living bread which has come down from
heaven.
Anyone who eats this bread will live forever;
and the bread I shall give
is my flesh, for the life of the world."

John 6:41-51

Jesus is significantly departing here from themes that he
has previously dealt with in his ministry, and he is significantly
departing from themes that we have dealt with in this consideration. Jesus is identifying himself the object of human longing and
desire not only in terms of our physical-biological hunger for
food but also in terms of our hunger for meaning, our hunger for
fulfillment, and our hunger for love. Jesus is situating himself as
the fulfillment of all of our human hungers. The human hungers
he directs himself to are physical, biological, sexual, personal,
social, emotional, psychological, intellectual, and spiritual. He
departs here in that he is saying that "the bread that I shall give
is my flesh, for the life of the world" (John 6:51).

Then the Jews started arguing with one another: "How can
this man give us his flesh to eat?" they said. Jesus replied:
"I tell you most solemnly,
if you do not eat the flesh of the Son of Man
and drink his blood,
you will not have life in you.
You who eat my flesh and drink my blood
have eternal life,
and I shall raise you up on the last day.
For my flesh is real food
and my blood is real drink.
You who eat my flesh and drink my blood
live in me

and I live in you.
As I, who am sent by the living Father,
myself draw life from the Father,
so whoever eats me will draw life from me.
This is the bread come down from heaven—
not like the bread our ancestors ate;
they are dead,
but anyone who eats this bread will live forever."

John 6:52-58

Jesus here unifies and resolves the various realities involved in human hunger and thirst in himself, his flesh and his blood. Jesus here offers to humanity his flesh and his blood to eat. In his offering of his own body and blood to humanity to eat he offers himself, his very person. "You who eat my flesh and drink my blood have eternal life." As Jesus said, "I am...life." Jesus offers food and drink: "My flesh is real food, and my blood is real drink." Jesus offers physical-biological food, bread and wine, and this satisfies our physical-biological hunger. This bread and this wine, the body, the flesh, and blood of Jesus satisfies the inner hunger and thirst for meaning and love and life. It is food for the person. It is food for the soul. "Whoever eats me will draw life from me." This flesh and blood of Jesus is who Jesus is. Jesus offers himself to us as real food.

After hearing it, many of his followers said, "This is intolerable language. How could anyone accept it?"
...after this, many of his disciples left him and stopped going with him.... Jesus said, "What about you, do you want to go away too?"

John 6:60, 66-67

QUESTIONS FOR PERSONAL AND COMMUNITY
REFLECTION AND DISCUSSION

1. Are you seeking the person of Jesus?

2. Recall an experience you have had where someone wasn't seeking you for who you were but simply wanted to use you.

3. What was the experience like for you of being used and manipulated?
   a. What feelings did this experience stir up in you?
   b. What reactions did you have toward the person who was relating to you like this?
   c. Did you feel rejected?

4. Is this feeling what Jesus experienced when the crowd followed him for more bread for their stomachs?

5. What is the deepest human hunger?

6. How others reject your deepest human hunger?

7. Do you reject this deepest human hunger in yourself?

8. How Jesus invite you to love your own emptiness and neediness for love?

9. Spend a prayer period considering this call of Jesus to you and to your sisters and brothers.

10. Share your experience in your group.

Chapter Five

The Sabbath Meal of the Scribes and Pharisees

As I wrote and rewrote this chapter I found that my writing style began to show me who the scribes and Pharisees were. I found myself writing very terse academic depictions of them. The style of these first pages is an excellent example of the epistemological principle: What you are coming to know determines the method (or style) by which you come to know it. In experiencing this with me, you can have some sense and feeling for what it must have been like for Jesus.

Now on a sabbath day he had gone for a meal to the house of the leading Pharisees; and they watched him closely. There in front of him was a man with dropsy, and Jesus addressed the scribes and Pharisees. "Is it against the law," he asked, "to cure a man on the sabbath, or not?" But they remained silent, so he took the man and cured him and sent him away. Then he said to them, "Which of you here, if his son falls into a well, or his ox, will not pull him out on a sabbath day without hesitation?" And to this they could find no answer.

Luke 14:1-6

Jesus chooses to share a meal with scribes and Pharisees at "the house of one of the leading Pharisees." Who were these people that Jesus wanted to share himself with? What were they like? I think answering these questions in a brief background investigation may prove helpful in understanding Jesus and bringing to light the significance of what is occurring.

Although the exact meaning of the word "Pharisee" is uncertain, it seems that it means "separated" or the "separate ones." Scholars seem to connect the origins of this sect or party within Judaism with the Hassidic sect of the Maccabean period some one hundred and fifty years before the birth of Christ. It seems that the Pharisees numbered some six thousand at the time of Christ. They understood Judaism as a religion whose central nature and obligation was a severe and strict observance of the law. They were legalistic rigorists, and in this they were very narrow. Their politics were flexible in that they preferred submission to Rome because Rome tolerated the religions of subjected peoples. The Pharisees were a lay group, as were the scribes, or lawyers, who were teachers and interpreters of the law.

The Pharisees opposed the common person of the land because the ignorant peasant from the country knew little of or cared little for the finer points of Pharisaic observance of the law. The Pharisees' observance of and adherence to the law and their idea of a nation-state religion was so strong that it alone survived the destruction of Jerusalem and the destruction of the Jewish community in Palestine by the Romans in the year 70 A.D. They believed in the existence of angels and spirits, the resurrection of the dead, and the last judgment. They subscribed to the belief that the law of Moses in the first five books of the Hebrew scriptures, the Torah, was to be surrounded and kept pure by the traditions of the elders which extended all the way back to Moses. All of these beliefs were denied by the Sadducees, another party at the time of Jesus, a priestly party from whom the chief priests came. What the Pharisees stood for and what they did ultimately was to depersonalize religion from an intimate relationship with God to an observance of exterior law. This relegated religion to a function, and centralized religion to ritual actions and the performance of prescriptions.

The Pharisees have an extended relationship with Jesus that is complex, intense, and virtually constant throughout his public life. They try to trap Jesus (Matthew 22:15). They are offended and outraged by Jesus' conduct. They are scandalized by Jesus' contact with publicans and sinners (Matthew 9:9), by his laxness of sabbath observance (Matthew 12:2), by his healing on the sabbath (Luke 14:1), and by his neglect of ritual ablutions (Matthew 15:1). They decry Jesus' claim of power to forgive sin (Luke 5:17). They accuse Jesus of being in league with Beelzebub when he casts out a devil (Matthew 12:24). They plot against the life of Jesus (Matthew 12:14). I think it is safe to say that they were hostile to Jesus because Jesus threatened their position of religious power over the people. With this brief background on who the Pharisees were, let us look at the experience of Jesus.

A Chill Up Your Spine

If we ask ourselves, "What was it like at this meal? What was it like for Jesus? What were the Pharisees like who invited Jesus to his house? What was the atmosphere like at table?" we need only to look at the end of the first sentence of the text for our answer: "They watched him closely." The "they" here refers to the Pharisees and lawyers who were seated at table with Jesus. "They watched him closely." When you hear that, how does it make you feel? If you are like me it will send a chill up your spine in a way that would make you wince in fear. It makes one feel uncomfortable to say the least. Have you ever been "watched closely"? What it tends to do to most of us is inhibit our natural spontaneity, our naturalness, in a way that we simply "are not ourselves" under those circumstances. What is going on here? What is going on is that human beings have a deep need for trust in order to grow. What this means is that from our very infancy we need an environment that we perceive to be safe and nurturing, accepting, encouraging, and loving in order for us to feel safe enough to be ourselves.

Trust Is a Prerequisite

We need to be provided with a sense of physical, emotional, and personal safety before we will allow ourselves to be. We need to trust before we can give ourselves over. We need to trust the environment. We need to trust the individuals around us before we will give ourselves over to them. It is correct to say that we have a need to trust because without the meeting of this need there is no giving over of ourselves. Trust is a prerequisite. When our environment feels unsafe, when the people around us threaten our physical, emotional, or personal safety and well-being, we are afraid. The fear that an individual feels then absorbs so much emotional and attentional energy that it tends to dominate his or her consciousness. Once this occurs, an individual generally does not have the emotional and attentional energy "to do or be his or her real self." We normally refer to this as "being inhibited" or "not being spontaneous." We say, "You are not being yourself" or "You are not free to be yourself." It is some of this that I believe we feel when we are "watched closely."

It's No Fun!

When you are "watched closely" in this sense it is generally by people who are attempting to do you some harm. They are "out to get you" and they are "looking for a way to get you." So they watch you closely to find a mistake in what you are doing or saying so that it can be used as information or proof to "do you in" or harm you. This is a threat or an attack on who we are. We react to protect ourselves or fight back. This absorbs our energy in a way that often leaves us without the energy we need to "be ourselves." It's no fun! We are "put on the defensive." We are stalked as prey. If we need trust, a feeling that "out there" is safe in order to be our spontaneous selves, and we feel that "out there" is unsafe and threatening, we lose the presence of our spontaneous free self. This is a real loss for us, and the reactions we have are grief, sorrow, and anger.

In contemplating the interior experience of Jesus during this meal that he shared with the scribes and Pharisees this element of pain emerges as real. Jesus chooses to share a meal with them. He chooses to break bread with them. He chooses them as companions. He chooses to share who he is with them. He chooses to have conversation with them. As he extends himself and offers himself to those present he is "watched closely." He is not received joyfully and accepted as gift and celebrated. He is "watched closely" with guarded, defensive, hostility. His overture of self-giving is met with aggression that is veiled and passive: "they remained silent." No response is a response! In this situation it is a deepening of the "watched closely" response. Jesus' sharing of who he is thus is perceived not as a gift to be enjoyed but as a threatening ominous loss to the identity and personal well-being of the Pharisees. Jesus is taking over. Jesus is attractive. Jesus has personal appeal. Jesus has personal power. Jesus has power to cure. "I don't," says the complex we have come to call "the self" of the Pharisee.

The responses of the Pharisees to their own interior perception of Jesus is loss, then fear of the loss, then anger at such a loss. Jesus is perceived as a robber, someone who is taking away from them what they dearly need, want, and desire. In essence, the Pharisees dearly wanted the admiration, love, esteem, and attention of the people. They wanted power over them. Jesus had this, and because he did he showed them that they really did not have what they so sorely craved. Their anger at Jesus so disorganized their own interior life and perception of themselves that they perceived Jesus as an enemy, an attacker, a robber, a threat to their sense of well-being. Jesus was an enemy. So, then, they must be enemies of Jesus.

Jesus as Enemy

As this meal progressed this sense of Jesus as enemy progressed, and the reaction of the Pharisees deepened. As Jesus shared more and more of who he was and what he was about, the experience he was faced with was an ever deepening rejection. Jesus perceived the pressure. He experienced here what he had spoken of in other hostile environments: "He did not work many miracles there because of their lack of faith" (Matthew

13:58). Jesus must have experienced a growing sense of uncomfortableness and isolation that turned this joyous event into work, into labor, and into a painful disintegrating experience. His love was not being accepted. These people were enemies.

Jesus Is Practicing What He Preaches

What we are looking at is Jesus choosing to share a meal with his enemies. Jesus is sharing his person, his companionship, with his enemies. He is sharing his convictions, his beliefs, his feelings, his desires, and his experience with his enemies. He is having a conversation with his enemies. He is telling his story to them. Jesus is loving his enemies. Jesus is not afraid to love his enemies. He may experience fear when he loves his enemies, but he is not allowing his fear to paralyze him to such an extent that he changes his behavior and does not share his love with his enemies. Jesus calls out to his enemies here. He makes a conscious choice to go out to his enemies. He intentionally shares a meal with them. What Jesus is doing is what he has enjoined us to do, when he said,

Love your enemies, do good to those who hate you, bless those who curse you, pray for those who treat you badly. To the one who slaps you on one cheek, present the other cheek too; to the one who takes your cloak from you, do not refuse your tunic. Give to everyone who asks you, and do not ask for your property back from the one who robs you. Treat others as you would like them to treat you. If you love those who love you, what thanks can you expect? Even sinners love those who love them. And if you do good to those who do good to you, what thanks can you expect? For even sinners do that much. And if you lend to those from whom you hope to receive, what thanks can you expect? Even sinners lend to sinners to get back the same amount. Instead, love

your enemies and do good, and lend without any
hope of return. You will have a great reward, and
you will be sons and daughters of the Most High, for
he himself is kind to the ungrateful and the wicked.

Luke 6:27-35

Who can help but feel so challenged after this injunction
given by Jesus as to be shaken to the very depths of one's being?
Who can stand up to this call of Jesus? "None of us" is the
answer. The ground of our joy is that "what God has begun in
us God will bring to completion" (Philippians 1:6). Our joy is
that we can come to our God who enjoins us to "love our enemies" and receive the strength to do this. Our gift is that we are
called to love with the love of God: "Be perfect as your heavenly
Father is perfect" (Matthew 5:48).

Love your enemies...in this way you will be children
of your Father in heaven, for he causes his sun to rise
on the bad as well as the good, and his rain to fall on
the honest as well as the dishonest alike.

Matthew 5:45

We are blessed in having Jesus to look at and contemplate
and desire strength from. Jesus is definitely loving his enemies
here. Jesus is spending time with people who don't like him and
don't accept him. Jesus is "practicing what he preaches."

Keep Your Eyes on Jesus

We need to keep our eyes on Jesus here. Jesus is the real
food that we need to love. It is in looking at and contemplating
this action of Jesus loving the scribes and Pharisees that we will
find the strength, love and power to love our enemies. It is only
in God's love in Jesus that we will find the wherewithal to do
this. It is quite obvious that we do not have it of ourselves to
love like this. And it will be quite obvious that if we do love like

this we will be loving with the love of God. As the phrase goes, "They'll know we are Christians by our love."

Jesus deepens his sharing of who he is with the Pharisees. He immerses himself in conversation with them at this meal. "He then told the guests a parable, because he had noticed how they picked the places of honor" (Luke 14:7).

> Then he said to his host, "When you give a lunch or a dinner, do not ask your friends, brothers, relations or rich neighbors, for fear they repay your courtesy by inviting you in return. No; when you have a party, invite the poor, the crippled, the lame, the blind; that they cannot pay you back means that you are fortunate, because repayment will be made to you when the virtuous rise again."
>
> Luke 7:12-14

Jesus is stating what he himself is doing. Jesus is verbally expressing who it is that he is inviting to his table to share a meal. Jesus is saying that he is sharing a meal with "the poor, the crippled, the lame, the blind." These are they whom Jesus is inviting to be his companions. It is these with whom the Lord wishes to share himself, his desires, feelings, convictions and dreams. It is these to whom he tells the story of himself. It is "the poor, the crippled, the lame, the blind" that the Lord wishes to listen to and make them feel listened to and loved. It is through this instruction that the Lord teaches the Pharisees the nature of their condition.

QUESTIONS FOR PERSONAL AND COMMUNITY REFLECTION AND DISCUSSION

1. Who are the scribes and Pharisees in your life?

2. Have you ever been intimidated by others? Recall those experiences.

3. Who does not trust you? How does that experience feel?

4. Who does trust you, and what does that feel like?

5. How do you relate to those in your life who do not trust you and who seek to intimidate you?

6. Who are your enemies?

7. How do you respond to your enemies? Do you love your enemies as Jesus does?

8. Bring your experience of your enemies before the Lord Jesus in prayer. Present yourself before Jesus as he relates to the scribes and Pharisees during this gospel meal. As you do this, repeat the words of Jesus as a mantra:

   Love your enemies. Do good to those who persecute you.

9. Share your experience with your group.

Chapter Six

Dining with the Rich: Zacchaeus

He entered Jericho and was going through the town
when a man whose name was Zacchaeus made his
appearance; he was one of the senior tax collectors
and a wealthy man. He was anxious to see what kind
of man Jesus was, but he was too short and could not
see him for the crowd; so he ran ahead and climbed a
sycamore tree to catch a glimpse of Jesus who was to
pass that way. When Jesus reached the spot he
looked up and spoke to him: "Zacchaeus, come
down. Hurry, because I must stay at your house
today." And he hurried down and welcomed him
joyfully. They all complained when they saw what
was happening. "He has gone to stay at a sinner's
house," they said. But Zacchaeus stood his ground
and said to the Lord, "Look, sir, I am going to give
half my property to the poor, and if I have cheated
anybody I will pay him back four times the amount."
And Jesus said to him, "Today salvation has come to
this house, because this man too is a son of Abraham;
for the Son of Man has come to seek out and save
what was lost."

Luke 19:1-10

> *A Spa for the Rich and Famous*

Jericho is the oldest continually inhabited city on the face
of the earth. This is quite a statement when you think about it.

Its foundation dates from the year 7000 B.C. It also is the lowest city on earth, being over some 750 feet below sea level. What made Jericho such a desirable place to live was its climate. It is warm and mild in the winter and tropical in the summer. Jericho is an oasis in the classical sense. There is a natural year-round spring of fresh water there yielding one thousand gallons per minute. A complex system of gravity flow irrigation brings the water to orchards of fruit trees and beds of flowers. Over the millennia Jericho was never urbanized as it was always used by conquering kings, sultans, or emperors as a personal villa. So its history is one of being a spa for the rich and famous.

Jericho is strategically located in that it lies as a gateway to one of the two main thoroughfares to Jerusalem. If one were coming from Galilee or from the north one would most likely come through Jericho, since the terrain in that direction is very level, following the Jordan River south. At Jericho, however, one begins a sharp ascent of some three thousand feet to Jerusalem. In any event these details highlight two characteristics given to us about Zacchaeus. He was a rich man, and he was a tax collector. Whether one was the result of the other we do not know. In Jericho it is possible that they could have been independent realities, although they obviously influenced each other.

Jericho was a place for the rich, and Jericho was a natural place to collect highway taxes and the like. This is the environment to which Zacchaeus accustomed himself. Jesus, as Luke presents him, is "on the road to Jerusalem." In this journey from Galilee in the north Jesus has been instructing his disciples that he "is destined to suffer grievously, to be rejected by the elders and chief priests and scribes and to be put to death, and to be raised up on the third day" (Luke 9:22). Jesus has taken the southerly route along the Jordan River on his way to Jerusalem to celebrate the Pasch with his disciples for the last time. So Jesus enters Jericho on the way to Jerusalem with his disciples.

Singing the Psalms of Ascent

There was a large crowd accompanying Jesus, as the previous encounter with Jesus outside Jericho indicates. Here Jesus gives the blind beggar, Bartimaeus, his sight. The large size of the crowd along "the road to Jerusalem" is occasioned by the yearly pilgrimage of the Jewish population to celebrate the Passover festival in Jerusalem. The whole people were on a pilgrimage, so there is a spirit of joy and festivity as they walk and ride their way slowly toward Jerusalem. As they would journey along their way, there would be much talk among themselves and much spontaneous breaking into the singing of various psalms, especially Psalm 122:

> How I rejoiced when they said to me,
> "Let us go to the house of Yahweh!"
> ...the tribes come...
> they come to praise Yahweh's name.
>
> Psalm 122:1, 4

The mood of the pilgrim Jewish people would have changed as different cantors intoned any one of the fifteen psalms of ascent, Psalm 120 through Psalm 134. The psalms of ascent are so named because they were sung as the Hebrew people journeyed to Jerusalem for the celebration of the Passover festival. Psalm 130, for example, pleads:

> From the depths I call to you, Yahweh.
> Lord, listen to my cry for help!
> Listen compassionately to my pleading!
> If you never overlooked our sins, Yahweh,
> Lord, could anyone survive?
> But you do forgive us: and for that we revere you.
>
> Psalm 130:1-4

One can hear the crowd respond to the singing of a pilgrim Psalm 133:

How good, how delightful it is
for all to live together like brothers and sisters:
fine as oil on the head...
where Yahweh confers his blessing, everlasting life.

Psalm 133:1-3

This is the scene as Jesus enters the lush, palm, sycamore, and fruit tree oasis of Jericho. As he is making his way through the town Luke tells us that a rich man named Zacchaeus "made his appearance." "He was anxious to see what kind of a man Jesus was." In general, people who are rich are used to getting their own way. They have things the way they want to have them. They get what they want. Zacchaeus was a rich man. Zacchaeus got what Zacchaeus wanted. So, seeing that the crowd was a large one and knowing that he was short in stature, Zacchaeus runs ahead to where he knows Jesus will pass. He climbs a sycamore tree where he can have a plain view of Jesus from close quarters without being blocked by anyone who may be taller than he is. He shows some initiative, creativity, self-knowledge, and enlightened self-interest concerning the meeting of his own needs. It is an attitude of the rich that there isn't a problem that they can't solve. It is a "can do" attitude and approach.

When Jesus reached the spot he looked up and spoke to him: "Zacchaeus, come down. Hurry, because I must stay at your house today." And he hurried down and welcomed him joyfully.

Luke 19:5-6

Jesus is surrounded by a crowd of people here. All kinds of people are massing around him, and Jesus chooses one of them. He chooses a rich man. Jesus chooses Zacchaeus out of the crowd. He chooses to stay at the home of a rich person. Jesus reaches out to the rich; he honors the rich with his presence. If we stop to think about it, when someone asks to stay at your home and to be your guest, this means that a meal will be involved.

They Did Not Like the Choice Jesus Was Making

It is not just "room" but "room and board" that Jesus is saying he wants here. Jesus is picking out of the crowd a rich man and saying to him, "I want to stay at your home with you today. I want to share a meal with you. I want to share myself with you." Anyone would know that all this is implicit in such a request. The crowd around Jesus knew this also. This is why they reacted as they did.

> They all complained when they saw what was happening. "He has gone to stay at a sinner's house," they said. But Zacchaeus stood his ground and said to the Lord, "Look, sir, I am going to give half my property to the poor, and if I have cheated anybody I will pay him back four times the amount." And Jesus said to him, "Today salvation has come to this house, because this man too is a son of Abraham; for the Son of Man has come to seek out and save what was lost."
>
> Luke 19:7-10

The crowd did not like the choice Jesus was making. They knew Zacchaeus was a rich man, and they knew Zacchaeus was a tax collector. They considered Zacchaeus to be a sinner. The crowd complains and complains loudly. Zacchaeus responds in amazing fashion, saying that he is going to give away half of his property to the poor, and that if he has gained any of his financial holdings by cheating anyone, he will give that amount back to them with the interest of a fourfold return. This is an amazing statement. It is a conversion of deep magnitude. Jesus responds by saying that "salvation has come to this house." Salvation indeed has come to this house as Jesus follows Zacchaeus' lead to his home. Jesus enters the home of Zacchaeus and shares a meal with him. Jesus stays at Zacchaeus' home "eating and drinking" what Zacchaeus has for him.

We can imagine what this meal was like. It was surely prepared in haste in that the cooks and housekeepers of Zacchaeus had no prior knowledge of the coming of Jesus to their master's residence. Presuming Zacchaeus was married, his wife had no knowledge of whom her husband was going to bring home for dinner that day. So I'm sure that as Zacchaeus swung open the front door of his home and proudly announced to all that Jesus of Nazareth was going to stay in his home, a burst of activity probably ensued. "Kill the fatted calf" or such similar instructions were probably issued by Zacchaeus as he tried to make sure his guest was comfortable while at the same time he organized the best possible performance from his staff of servants to ensure the best possible cuisine for a meal that really wasn't expected. Although it was a surprise for the household, we can assume that the meal he provided was more than adequate. Those servants who knew Zacchaeus were fully capable of seeing in his countenance how special was the event. They responded with dispatch and diligence to the importance of the situation as seen in Zacchaeus' face. I think we could say Jesus was treated royally with the best this rich man could offer.

Jesus Chooses the Rich To Be with Him

Jesus chose to share a meal with the rich in a rich house with rich food served by a rich person's servants. Jesus sought this out. Jesus sought out the rich on the rich person's own terms—in a rich house with rich surroundings in the context of an opulent meal, "for the Son of Man has come to seek out and save what was lost" (Luke 19:10). Jesus chooses this rich man, Zacchaeus, to be his companion: he breaks bread with him. Jesus chose to share himself with the rich, someone who had all that the world could offer. Jesus shared his story with the rich. Jesus chose to share his feelings, his desires, his convictions, his thoughts, his reflections, and his very self with the rich. Jesus chose this rich man to listen to. Jesus had conversation with the rich, and in this conversation Zacchaeus was converted.

In Jesus' taking time to seek out what was lost, Zacchaeus

was converted. "Today salvation has come to this house," Jesus says. Zacchaeus listens to Jesus, receives him, accepts who he is, and changes his life: "I am going to give half my property to the poor, and if I have cheated anybody I will pay him back four times the amount" (Luke 19:8). Zacchaeus is "living as Jesus lived." Zacchaeus is talking and acting as Jesus talks and acts: "he emptied himself" (Philippians 1). Zacchaeus is "imitating" Christ. His life was changed as Jesus shared a meal with him. Jesus was breaking bread, inviting him to be his companion, and sharing himself with him in conversation. Jesus sought him out and chose to stay with him in his house. Jesus chose to share a meal with him. Jesus invited him.

Look at all that happened at the meal Jesus had with Zacchaeus. Look at all the real food, all of the intimacy, all of the satisfaction, and all of the fulfillment. This is the real food of Jesus.

QUESTIONS FOR PERSONAL AND COMMUNITY REFLECTION AND DISCUSSION

1. What is your attitude toward the rich?

2. What is your attitude toward money?

3. Are you possessed by wealth in that it dominates you by attraction or by repulsion?

4. Are you strongly attracted by those who have money? Or are you strongly repulsed by those who have a great deal of financial resources?

5. Does money make a difference to you?
   a. Do you "complain" about those who have money, or do you look for their "ungifted" aspects?
   b. Can you celebrate their giftedness and give thanks?

6. Bring these people and your relationships with them into your prayer of contemplating the gospel scene of Jesus and Zacchaeus. Be straightforward about yourself with Jesus.

7. Share your experience in your group.

8. Being "rich" is a category that can apply to many other aspects of human life besides the area of finance. Human beings can be rich in talents, intellectuality, sensitivity, imagination, beauty, personality, and many other areas. What is your attitude toward those who are rich in these gifts?

9. Share these reactions in your group.

Chapter Seven

At Table with a Woman

In our culture, scientific accuracy is a value. It is highly prized. With the invasion of the computer and computer chip technology we cannot escape the realization that scientific accuracy is the very air we breathe. It is virtually a requirement now for an entry level job to be able to operate a computer. This is our world, and if it is not now your environment it very quickly will be. The whole world is being touched by this. Human science has influenced us and the way we think.

We need to look at this in ourselves because it affects the way we look at the scriptures which are a primary source of this consideration. We tend to look at the biblical texts that the tradition of the church has handed down to us with an historically critical eye that says: "Just give me the facts. What actually happened? Who actually did what? Where? When did it happen?" The answers to these questions will give us the truth that the scriptures have to give us. That there is merit in this approach goes without saying. The kind of distinguishing that goes on in such an approach is often rewarded with rich, abundant, and clarifying insight and grace. The modern biblical movement is a joyful and glowing monument to this. What modern biblical scholarship has unearthed with its own critical style and method is the fact that the texts of the scriptures come from a society and culture very different from ours. The authors of the scriptures had, for the most part, a very different mindset than we do. The way they communicated and expressed the values that they held dear was different from the way we do.

What modern biblical scholarship is telling us is that the

authors of scripture did not have the type of historical concern and preoccupation for scientific factual accuracy that we have today. Their concern was to proclaim the word of God. And, more specifically, in the New Testament, their concern was to preach the gospel, the good news of Jesus, the Christ.

We are presented with a type of problem that centuries-old tradition in the church has given us. There is an implied recognition that the woman who was a public sinner, a prostitute, and the woman who washed the feet of Jesus with her tears and who wiped them with her hair during the meal at Simon the Pharisee's house was the same woman who was Martha and Lazarus' sister at Bethany. This is also the same woman who stood with Mary, the mother of Jesus, at the foot of the cross. This is the same woman who went to anoint the body of Jesus as it lay in the tomb after the crucifixion, and this is the same woman to whom Jesus appeared in the garden after his resurrection: Mary Magdalene. Modern biblical scholarship tells us, without going into each exegetical raison d'être, that it was not the same woman who experienced all of these events. These findings do not preclude or vitiate a certain grace that emanated from the tradition of the church that identified all of these women into one and the same person: Mary of Magdala. I would like to take in the elements of this tradition without violating them and yet respecting modern biblical findings.

> One of the Pharisees invited him to a meal. When he arrived at the Pharisee's house and took his place at table, a woman came in, who had a bad name in the town. She had heard he was dining with the Pharisee and had brought with her an alabaster jar of ointment. She waited behind him at his feet, weeping, and her tears fell on his feet, and she wiped them away with her hair; then she covered his feet with kisses and anointed them with the ointment.

> When the Pharisee who had invited him saw this he said to himself, "If this man were a prophet, he

would know who this woman is that is touching him and what a bad name she has." Then Jesus took him up and said, "Simon, I have something to say to you." "Speak, Master," was the reply. "There was once a creditor who had two men in his debt; one owed him five hundred denarii, the other fifty. They were unable to pay, so he pardoned them both. Which of them will love him more?" "The one who was pardoned more, I suppose," answered Simon. Jesus said, "You are right."

Then he turned to the woman. "Simon," he said. "You see this woman? I came into your house, and you poured no water over my feet, but she has poured out her tears over my feet and wiped them away with her hair. You gave me no kiss, but she has been covering my feet with kisses ever since I came in. You did not anoint my head with oil, but she has anointed my feet with ointment. For this reason I tell you that her sins, her many sins, must have been forgiven her, or she would not have shown such great love. It is the one who is forgiven little who shows little love." Then he said to her, "Your sins are forgiven." Those who were with him at table began to say to themselves, "Who is this man, that he even forgives sins?" But he said to the woman, "Your faith has saved you; go in peace."

Luke 7:36-50

Jesus has accepted an invitation from one of the Pharisees, Simon, to share a meal together. In this acceptance Jesus has extended an invitation of his own to those with whom he is to dine. This invitation of Jesus is to deepen through the events that are to occur during the meal. These events that occur during the meal amount to the very substance of what Jesus wants to share with those at table: his very self.

The Context Was a Meal

As the gospel writer of Luke gives us the experience of Jesus he begins by stating the context of this event. It is a meal. Jesus chooses to share a meal with Simon the Pharisee. In the midst of this meal a woman who was a sinner in the eyes of all present breaks into the occasion. We don't know the nature of the sin of this woman. What we do know is that this woman's sin was public. Most people at this meal knew her and knew her sin. It was common knowledge. It could very well have been that this woman was a prostitute in the town where this meal took place. It could have been that this woman had married a man who was an outcast, a publican or a tax collector and publicly supported him. Or it could have been that this woman was living with a man outside of wedlock. Whatever the nature of her sin, we can be sure it was deep and ongoing, and, as a result, it had become public.

For Men Only

The significance of this meal experience for Jesus can be seen if we look at the circumstances in which Jesus finds himself. This meal was most certainly a "for men only" event. The meal was a sort of "get to know Jesus of Nazareth, his theology, his religious beliefs, and his religious policies" for Pharisees who were all male. It was a type of all-male religious club meal. If women were there it was in a role of meal server or "washer of hands" servant. Such servants would sit behind the men who were eating around the common horseshoe-shaped low-lying table of the day. Such female servants would be employed to be attentive to the needs of the Pharisees in such common meal occurrences as providing bread or wine or the entree of the meal. This woman who was a sinner in the town could very likely have made her way into such an "inner sanctum" with the female servants for such a meal. She also could have gone somewhat unnoticed to a position immediately behind Jesus. This could very easily have occurred as the meal began with all present being intent on the motif "What are the religious and political beliefs of Jesus?" Jesus assumed the normal position of the day in dining by reclining somewhat before the low-lying meal table. This position allowed for his feet to be tucked behind him. This is where this woman positioned herself. The gospel writer puts it, "She waited behind him at his feet" (Luke 7:38).

The Ache of Weeping Rose

All of this could have transpired in a way that went unnoticed. What follows could not have been. This woman began to weep. Probably she wept quietly at first, then deeply. She surrendered to her sorrow, for "her tears fell on his feet." This, little by little, began to make an encroachment upon the intentive interests of the Pharisees. They were interrupted and uncomfortably distracted from their pursuit by something that was "out of order." Something unplanned was happening. There was a woman behind Jesus, and she was crying. She was more than crying—she was weeping. And her weeping had such a genuine quality about it that it had power. It had such power as to be absorbing to anyone who heard her and saw her. One could not now not hear her. Her tears commanded attention. Her human honesty broke through the calculated pretense of those at table in a way that disarmed them. Those at table were caught up before they could defend themselves. They were stopped without knowing how, without knowing what was happening. A silence dawned on those at table as the ache of weeping rose, as the sound of tears falling filled the room.

Seduced by Honesty

A crushing sense of distance and gratitude resolved in her as she abandoned her forehead to his feet and wiped her tears away with her hair. She kissed his feet again and again, over and over. A rage began to fill the room. The Pharisees became angry that they had been seduced by honesty. There was a hostile denial that each had been attracted to the power of such simple beauty. The Pharisees were angry that this woman had power. She had power that they did not have.

She began to anoint his feet with ointment. The fragrance was fought by the Pharisees. It didn't exist. She didn't exist. What they heard and saw and perceived and smelled wasn't real. It wasn't powerful. This is the woman who is a sinner. This woman has a bad reputation in the town. This is what must be seen. This is what must be focused on. A quick refocusing driven by spontaneous anger affects those at table with a certain all-embracing suddenness.

> If this man were a prophet, he would know who this woman is that is touching him and what a bad name she has.
>
> Luke 7:39

The unexpressed following implication is obvious! And, therefore, he would tell her to get away from him, for she is unclean because she is a sinful woman. He would tell her not to touch him, and tell her to get out immediately because her very presence is defiling him and the rest of those at table. Her touch of him is defiling him to such a degree that he himself now needs to leave the meal table and himself become an outcast until he is cleansed by ritual ablutions.

| Jesus Reveals His Identity to the Pharisees |

Jesus, reclining at this meal with the Pharisees, begins to share the truth of who he is with those at table. He has a conversation with them. He tells the story of who he is to them there at table during this meal. He shares his values, his feelings, his convictions, and his sense of self with them. Jesus says:

"Simon, I have something to say to you." "Speak, Master," was the reply. "There was once a creditor who had two men in his debt; one owed him five hundred denarii, the other fifty. They were unable to pay, so he pardoned them both. Which of them will love him more?" "The one who was pardoned more, I suppose," answered Simon. Jesus said, "You are right." Jesus then turned to the woman. "Simon," he said. "You see this woman."

Luke 7:41-44

Jesus here deepens his sharing of himself with those who were at table with him for a meal. Jesus recognizes the presence of this woman. There is much more involved here in this recognition. It is not a recognition of "this woman." It is that Jesus at table, sharing a meal with the Pharisees, recognizes "a woman." It is the recognition of a woman that Jesus is sharing with those at table as food. The fact that Jesus acknowledged the presence of a woman at the table of the Pharisees was looked upon by those at table as an insult. In the ancient Near East women had few rights as free persons. A woman was subject to a man, either her father or her husband. Under the law women had an inferior position to men and were treated so as to adultery, divorce, dowry, family, inheritance, prostitution, and widowhood. Socially, women had a lower position. In Exodus 20:17, a wife is listed among the property of a man. The work of women in the time of Jesus seems to have been long and hard, including milling, baking, spinning, weaving, sewing, care of the house, and raising children. Women also shared in the tilling of the soil, plowing, sowing, reaping and threshing.

Jesus Loved Her

It seems that women did not generally eat with men (Genesis 18:9; Ruth 2:14). It was definitely the case in this situation. This fact brings to light the importance of what Jesus is doing: turning toward this woman, acknowledging her, and bringing her presence into the conversation there at table with the Pharisees. This was not done. Jesus did it. Jesus shared himself with this woman who was a public sinner during this meal by receiving her, by receiving who she was, by receiving her expression of affection. He brought her into the meal by acknowledging her presence and accepting her love. He loved her. In this he shared who he was with her, and in this he shared who he was with the scribes and Pharisees. In this he shared her with the Pharisees. He shared her love for him and his love for her. He shared their relationship with the Pharisees. In this Jesus shared the real food of this woman's life with the Pharisees. Jesus broke the bread of who this woman was with the Pharisees. The person this woman was became the food Jesus gave to the Pharisees. In this he broke the bread of who he was with them. In this he shared who he was with them: someone who passionately loves every person and someone who is loved. In sharing with the Pharisees, he fed them with real food: his love, his words, his example, his very self.

This real food is echoed in the first letter of John: "God is greater than our conscience" (1 John 3:20).

QUESTIONS FOR PERSONAL AND COMMUNITY REFLECTION AND DISCUSSION

1. Do women have an inferior position in your family? your school? your church? your office? your club? your social circle?

2. Do you categorize women or stereotype women in a way that does not place their humanity first?

3. Do you distinguish consciously your treatment of women on the grounds of gender?

4. Are you prejudiced (pre-judging) for or against women in

the area of work, academics, legal issues, intellectuality, or social interactions?

5. What are your issues surrounding gender?

6. What is the history of your family regarding this issue?

7. How were you brought up regarding this?

8. Who were the significant people in your family that formed your attitude toward women?

9. What were your early formative experiences regarding gender? Who was present?

10. Were those experiences joyful or painful? helpful or threatening?

11. See the love Jesus shares with the woman in this gospel scene. Place yourself in this biblical experience exactly as you are with your own issues of gender. Share your feelings and history with Jesus, with this woman, and with the Pharisee.

12. Share your experience in your group.

Chapter Eight

The Last Supper
with the Apostles

The day of Unleavened Bread came round, the day on which the Passover had to be sacrificed, and he sent Peter and John, saying, "Go and make the preparations for us to eat the Passover." "Where do you want us to prepare it?" they asked. "Listen," he said, "as you go into the city you will meet a man carrying a pitcher of water. Follow him into the house, and say to the owner of the house, 'The Master has this to say to you: Where is the dining room in which I can eat the Passover with my disciples?' The man will show you a large upper room furnished with couches. Make the preparations there." They set off and found everything as he had told them, and prepared the Passover.

Luke 22:7-13

Scripture scholars and biblical archaeologists tell us that this familiar story took place in the city of Jerusalem. More specifically, this meal took place in the Mount Zion area of the old city of Jerusalem. If you were to stand on the Mount of Olives and gaze at the city of Jerusalem over the Kidron Valley you would see some half mile away to your left, to the south, a hill slightly higher than the rest of the old city of Jerusalem. This high point of the old area of Jerusalem is known as Mount Zion. It is a small area, and at the time of Christ this was the area of the city that quartered a sect of Hebrew religious reformers known as the Essenes. It is pertinent to that full-scale members of the Essene community, such as the ones at Qumran, were celibate. This is significant because Jesus instructed his disciples to "go into the city and you will meet a man carrying a pitcher of water" (Luke 22:9). This would have been an unusual sight, as men never carried pitchers of water at that time. It was a woman's job and task to do so. If there was an all-male celibate community there in the city, a man would have to go and draw his own water. The instructions of Jesus to his disciples were somewhat easy to carry out, since it was easy to spot a man carrying a water jar because it was such a singular and rare occurrence. As we know from biblical scholarship that there was a community of Essenes at the time of the Lord on Mount Zion, it is a possibility that the last supper room was made available through some Essene contact for Jesus and his disciples.

Since the time of Christ, Christians have venerated the Mount Zion area as the site of the last supper. Throughout the centuries churches have been built there to commemorate this event.

So with the scene set in Jerusalem, we contemplate Jesus inviting his disciples to the banquet feast of the passover lamb. Jesus invites his disciples to dine with him. Jesus invites Peter, James, and John. Jesus invites Matthew, Simon called the Zealot, and Judas son of James, Andrew, the brother of Peter, Philip, Bartholomew, Thomas, James, the son of Alphaeus, and Judas Iscariot.

In the upper room...

They were at supper ... and he got up from table, removed his outer garment and, taking a towel, wrapped it round his waist; he then poured water into a basin and began to wash the disciples' feet and to wipe them with the towel he was wearing.

John 13:2-5

In the Power of Another

Jesus is sharing who he is in the context of a meal. Jesus is here giving the real food of who he is to those at table with him. Jesus is feeding those whom he has invited to his table with the real food of his personhood. He does this by the gesture of a servant, one who is in the power of another. He washes the feet of those with whom he has chosen to share a meal. It was the servant of the house who would wash the feet of the guest who had walked the dusty roads of Israel. It was the servant of the house who was at the disposal of the guest who was uncomfortable and needed to be tended to. Jesus identifies himself as that humble servant.

Treating a servant with disdain was so inbred that Peter said to Jesus as Jesus came to him to wash his feet, "Never! You shall never wash my feet" (John 13:8). Peter, knowing that Jesus was Master and Lord, would not tolerate Jesus serving him. The notion of Jesus taking on the role of a common servant was too much for Peter to endure. Yet Jesus does this. Jesus takes a towel and water and washes the feet of his disciples during the meal which he has invited them to. The discomfort of the apostles as Jesus did this to them at table could only be dealt with by the presence of Jesus himself washing and drying their feet. This washing and drying of their feet made them feel uncomfortable, and it was the personal love and presence of Jesus being fed to them during this that brought comfort, consolation, and deep peace resolving the pain of such an incongruity. Jesus serving them! Serving! Jesus was not asking to be served! The food of Christ's humble service is real and stunning to one's expectations.

The Inner Circle...Astonishing!

This meal experience draws us into itself as we gaze around the upper room watching Jesus. Who is there? Who is this inner circle of Jesus' chosen intimates? These men are fishermen from Galilee for the most part. Astonishing! They have no college education! They have no post-graduate degrees! They have no high school education by our standards! They have no high-bred business capability! They are not landed gentry! They are not well born!

These disciples of Jesus are the lowly. They are commoners, simple and good! They are not all that bright, yet Jesus is sharing who he is with them during this meal. Jesus values them. The love of God lifts them up. The love of God makes them who they are. And Jesus here takes the time during this meal to reveal to them the nature of who God is. Jesus serves them. Jesus serves the lowly and shares himself with the common person.

> When he had washed their feet and put on his clothes again he went back to the table. "Do you understand," he said, "what I have done to you? You call me Master and Lord, and rightly; so I am. If I, then, the Lord and Master, have washed your feet, you should wash each other's feet. I have given you an example so that you may copy what I have done to you…. Now that you know this, happiness will be yours if you behave accordingly."
>
> John 13:12-17

The Real Food of Happiness

This is the real food of happiness: to serve one another. Jesus feeds the lowly with the good things of his presence. This is the gift of real food, the way of happiness. This unfolding of who Jesus is will be Jesus' gift to all: the way, the truth, and the life. It is real food that Jesus is serving at this meal, and Jesus is serving the real food of who he is at this meal.

Within the setting of a meal Jesus deepens the gift he is giving those he has chosen to be his intimates. Jesus continues to feed his disciples with his selfhood. John presents to us what came from the loving presence of Jesus during that last supper. Five full chapters, Chapter 13 through Chapter 17, reveal to us the depth of the intimacy between Jesus and his apostles during the meal.

After dealing with Judas, Jesus begins to share with his apostles his words about his coming glorification. He begins his "farewell" to his disciples:

> I give you a new commandment:
> love one another;
> just as I have loved you,
> you also must love one another.
>
> John 13:34

Get the Picture

The newness of this commandment lies not in the injunction to "love one another." The newness lies in the following phrase, "as I have loved you." Jesus is here placing squarely on his own shoulders the very essence of holiness, and in so doing is taking the same responsibility from our own eager hands. Jesus is placing the source of all love in himself as was given him by his Father. What follows, then, is that we are not to use ourselves as the norm of love. Jesus is the norm of love; we are not that norm. We are not to love each other as we would have it. We are to love each other as Jesus has loved us. The origin and the source of our love is how Jesus has loved us, not how we love ourselves or one another. We simply need to begin to look around the table at who Jesus has invited to this intimacy to begin to "get the picture." We simply need to ask ourselves the simple question, "Whom does Jesus choose to share a meal with?" to get the answer. Jesus shared himself with country peasants from Cana, with Levi the tax collector, with the scribes and Pharisees, with Zacchaeus, with the rich man, with the sinful woman, and with Peter, James, and John, the fishermen.

"Love one another as I have loved you." Share yourself with others the way I have shared myself with you. This, indeed, is a new commandment as Jesus' love is new, as Jesus'

love seeks out the suffering and the lost as a shepherd seeks out
the lost sheep. Jesus shares his very life experience with his
apostles in this statement as he refers to his own "way" as the
very model and source of this love of which he now speaks.

John presents us with the prayer of Jesus during this last
meal of the Lord with his disciples.

Father, the hour has come:
glorify your Son
so that your Son may glorify you;
and, through the power over all that you have given
him,
let him give eternal life to all those
you have entrusted to him.
And eternal life is this:
to know you,
the only true God,
and Jesus Christ whom you have sent.
I pray for them.

John 17:1-3, 9

The Human Heart Finds Its Home

What is this power that the Father has given Jesus over all?
What is this eternal life? Jesus prays to his Father to allow him
ever more deeply to give this to his disciples and, indeed, to
everyone. The power and the eternal life that Jesus is speaking
of here is the passionate love of God. He is speaking of the love
God has for his people. This is the love who is God. Jesus is the
winner of hearts because of how he does things. Jesus is God
because he wins human hearts with love. Jesus is the first-born
of all creation because of how he wins human hearts. Jesus is the
first-born of all creation because he wins human hearts by love.
Jesus is the ruler and king of all creation because of his love and
because of the way he loves. To have this love in one's heart is to
have eternal life. To love with this love, the passionate love of

God, is to have eternal life. It is because God is love that "every knee will bend" (Philippians 2:10). It is in the love of Jesus that the human heart finds its meaning, its home, and its lover. This love is eternal. Finding it is finding eternal life. Jesus says this to his apostles, and prays that he can give this to his apostles. He does this during a meal:

> As you sent me into the world,
> I have sent them into the world.
> I pray not only for these,
> but for those also
> who through their words will believe in me.
> May they all be one.
> Father, may they be one in us,
> as you are in me and I am in you,
> so that the world may believe it was you who sent me.
> I have given them the glory you gave to me,
> that they may be one as we are one.
> With me in them and you in me,
> may they be so completely one
> that the world will realize that it was you who sent me,
> and that I have loved them as much as you loved me.
>
> John 17:18, 20-23

Jesus deepens and yearns his prayer and love down through the centuries here. He extends his presence in the world by sending his disciples in his love to every human being who hears his words through them. The phenomenon of missioning to the ministry of the love of God is born of the desire of Jesus as he looks at each of the disciples around the supper table. Jesus experiences all who will hear his words spoken by his ministers sent down the nights and down the days. Jesus' prayer is that all may be one in love. The love that Jesus is referring to is the love that the Father has for him. This is the love he is loving his disciples with. Jesus desires that they may love with this love and that all may experience this love through them.

I have made your name known to them
and will continue to make it known,
so that the love with which you loved me
may be in them,
and so that I may be in them.

John 17:26

Jesus desires to remain in the world with the ones he loves—his people. He sheds light on this intimacy here, saying:

I am the vine,
you are the branches....
Cut off from me you can do nothing.

John 15:5

The union of love here is so deep that only one who recognizes its origin and source can remain loving and being its messenger and conveying its presence. In this recognition comes power, as Jesus says:

If you remain in me
and my words remain in you,
you may ask what you will
and you shall get it.

John 15:7

This is an astounding statement. It is a statement that has confounded believers and non-believers, Christians and non-Christians for centuries. Jesus during this meal is sharing lovers' love. Jesus is saying that if you and I are the most important person in each other's lives, then ask what you will, and you will get it. Jesus is saying that if my love, the love I have received from my Father and pass on to you, is the very core of your being, the very heart of your person as it is mine, then ask what you will and you will get it because you are trustworthy. Your heart is in the right place. Your being is founded on my love. Your compass is guided by the right magnetism. I can give you what you ask, and you will be gentle with it, not abuse it, and you will not be consumed by it. You will not be co-opted by it in a way that you will be seduced into adoring it as an idol. This is because your whole life is my love.

As the Father has loved me,
so I have loved you.
Remain in my love.

John 15:9

The Core of Our Being Searches Out God's Love

Abiding in the love of God is having God's love as the very root and core of our being. This allows us to have God's viewpoint on all things. It brings us to be the presence of God's love in the world. One searches out God's love in every situation and circumstance. You seek out this love of God for every person you come in contact with. It is this preoccupation with the love of God that relegates everything else in our lives to be "everything else." This allows us to possess all things in God's love as God's love possesses all things—gently.

I have told you this
so that my own joy may be in you
and your joy be complete.
This is my commandment:
love one another,
as I have loved you.

John 15:11-12

It Is Possible for Us To Love

The power of the command of Jesus to love is rich in resources for us. The simple reason is that Jesus is the center of all creation, the Alpha and the Omega, that from whom all creation has come and to whom all creation will find its resolution and being. Jesus cannot ask us to do what is impossible. It is in following this command of Jesus that our joy will be complete. It is in the realization that "what God has begun he will bring to completion" (Philippians 1:6) that we will find our joy. It is in the realization that "the Lord Jesus Christ is Savior who transforms us into his own glorious body by virtue of that dynamism that enables him to subject everything to himself" (Philippians 3:20-21) that we will find joy. It is in the realization that Jesus cannot ask us to do the impossible that our joy will be full. Jesus has asked us to love as he has loved us. Since Jesus cannot ask us to do something that is impossible for us to do, it is possible for us to love with God's love. It is implicit in Jesus' asking that we can love ourselves and love others as he has loved us. Buried deep within the request of Jesus is the invitation of God, the grace of God, and the love of God to bring this request into a full reality in our lives.

Reality Perception: We Love with Human Love

It is a reality perception on our part to know that our own love is joyful and life-giving. It is also a reality perception on our part that we often, and even daily, come up short in loving ourselves and in loving those around us. This is who we are. We are human, and we love with human love. We know that, and because we love with human love, we suffer deep pain and embarrassment. The joy of the command of our God to us is that we are not locked into our own love and behavior as our only option. The joy of the command of Jesus to us at his last meal with his apostles is that we are called to love as he loved us. How can we do that? Can we love as Jesus loved us with our own love? No! We cannot because we are who we are. We can love as Jesus loved us and fulfill this command only by loving with the love of Jesus, that is, seeing with the eyes of Jesus, hearing with the ears of Jesus, being Jesus' hands on the earth, and being Jesus' voice here and now. Jesus is offering us his love to love with as a possibility, his grace to be with as a reality, his desire to desire with, and his yearning to yearn with. We can only fulfill this command if we love with the love of God.

Only in Loving with the Love of God

It is this that God is calling us to do. It is this that God offers to us. It is this love that God gives to us to love with if we turn and receive. Herein is the reason Jesus became one of us. It is only in loving with the love of God that we will be who we have always wanted to be. Our Creator and Lord knows who we are and who we have always wanted to be. It is in the love of God that he has not left us orphans but has come to give us "real food"—this love of God.

John has given over five full chapters of his work to what Jesus shared with his disciples during the meal. The riches here are powerful. The food that Jesus shared is satisfying. It refreshes the soul, the very core of our being. The washing of the feet of the disciples, the words of Jesus about his relationship with his Father, the parable of the vine and the branches, the words of Jesus concerning the world, the promise of sending the Spirit, the prayer of Jesus for us, the sending of us into the world, the body and the blood of Christ given as bread to eat and wine to drink are all immeasurable gifts. All of this is given to us during a meal. WHAT FOOD!!!

This is all realized and celebrated in the real food of the body and blood of Christ which Jesus shares with us. As we know, this supper of the Lord Jesus has its roots in ancient Hebrew history. And Jesus here fulfills this Old Testament experience in his own body and blood.

The Hebrew Passover meal was a sharing of the Passover lamb offered to Yahweh as a sacrifice of praise and thanksgiving. There was an offering and a sacrifice of the lamb. The blood of the lamb was painted on the doorposts of the homes of the Hebrew people in Egyptian exile. Through the blood of the lamb they were "passed over" by the angel of death who destroyed the first-born of each Egyptian household. This blood of the lamb freed the people of God.

The Hebrew people then roasted the lamb and shared the lamb in a meal. They sealed their covenant as an agreement with God by this covenant meal. It was a celebration and a consummation meal. It was a covenant meal. The eating of the Passover meal together sealed their covenant as an agreement with God that they would be a community of God's people.

Jesus celebrates the Passover meal with his disciples. Jesus here shares the real food of his body and blood. This meal was a blessing, in Hebrew a berakah. In the passion, death, and resurrection that he is about to endure, he fulfills the Old Testament sacrifice of the lamb. In the eucharistic sacrament of his body and blood given as bread and wine, Jesus fulfills the sealing of the covenant agreement between God and the people. The covenant agreement between God and the human race is now made in the eucharistic body and blood of Christ.

Something To Celebrate

The apostles share in the body and blood of Jesus, and Jesus directs the apostles to share his body and blood with every person in the human community. In this communion meal we are sealed as God's people: a covenanted community. This is real food. This is something to celebrate. This is what the eucharist is: the real food of the sense of security of being God's own loved ones.

> I give you a new commandment:
> love one another;
> just as I have loved you,
> you also must love one another.
> By this love you have for one another,
> everyone will know that you are my disciples.
>   John 13:34

Jesus leaves the people he loves so dearly with his presence and his love. This is so clear to Jesus that he says that people will know it is he as they observe us. They will see Jesus in us. They will know that it is the love of God in us as they see us live. People will know this because of what they see us do. They will know this because what we do will be to love where there is no love, to give where there is no return, to be present where there is need but no call. This is God-like. This is seeking out the lost with understanding and love. Only God would do this. Only the love of God would pursue so strongly. Only God would be so patient. Only God would be so kind. Only God would be so enduring in the face of obstacles. Only God's love would be so present. The people are right! Jesus sends his presence and love forth into the world as he was sent. He sends his love forth into the world present in the hearts of men and women. These are passionate with love as he is loving.

Everyone will know it is Jesus.

QUESTIONS FOR PERSONAL AND COMMUNITY REFLECTION AND DISCUSSION

1. Is your being founded on the love of God? What does that mean? Share your responses in your group.

2. Spend time in contemplating this gospel scene of Jesus with the apostles. Gently allow yourself the freedom to simply watch Jesus wash the feet of the apostles and your own feet. Allow your own reactions to simply be within you. Hear Jesus reveal to you and to all present the words of eternal life, who Jesus is.

3. Share your responses in your group.

4. Are you accustomed to share who you are with others during your own experience of eating with someone else?

5. What is your experience of service? Whom do you serve?
    What is the experience like for you? Can you bring this
    before Jesus, who is washing your feet?

6. Experience Jesus saying to you and to everyone present that
    you are to be his presence in the world down through the
    centuries.

7. Reflect on your feelings.
    a. What does this stir up in you?
    b. How do you feel?
    c. What are you experiencing?
    d. Share this with your group.

8. What does it mean for you to love with the love of God?
    Share your response in your group.

9. What does it mean to you that Jesus shared so much of who
    he is during a meal?

10. Share your reactions in your group.

Chapter Nine

Real Food:
The Risen Jesus

The cenacle room on Mount Zion is the eleventh century crusader upper room that commemorates the last supper of the Lord with the apostles. As you can imagine, there are many people who go on pilgrimage there and pray. As we pray over the scriptural events that occurred in the upper room it is surprising to find that so much went on while they were there at table having a meal.

The resurrection accounts show how the apostles were filled with joy when the risen Jesus appeared to them as they were eating. As Luke recounts it, "They were beside themselves with joy" (Luke 24:20).

As we contemplate the joy of those present, what spontaneously occurs is that we say that this is what we want also. We want this joy. As we look around the room in our contemplation we begin to realize that those present were joyful to the degree to which they had seen Jesus suffer his death on the cross of Calvary. There was a relationship! Those who had abandoned Christ on his cross and had heard from others that he had died on Calvary were joyful at seeing Jesus resurrected. This was true. But those who had stayed with Jesus as he died his agonizing death on the cross of Calvary had a deeper joy in their hearts as they saw him resurrected standing before them in the upper room. It is this deeper joy that we want. It is this deeper joy that we seek.

| *There Lies a Recommitment Here* |

As we in the community of believers contemplate this experience of the risen Jesus, the faces of those people in our lives who are suffering from events that reveal a vicious world come into our consciousness. The grace of God brings this reality into our consciousness: Jesus is suffering his death on the cross in the suffering of my broken brothers and sisters. This is happening even in those who are closest to us or with whom we live. We have a chance. We have the opportunity not to abandon Christ on the cross. We have the chance to have this joy of the resurrection by being with Christ on Calvary. We can stand by these people, Christ suffering, as they hang on their cross and, by comforting them, comfort Christ. Then we will have the deeper joy that we wish for. We have a chance. There lies a recommitment here to work with a deeper love and dedication and urgency.

What is remarkable about the joy of those present in the upper room is that it occurred while they were "at table." As the scripture has it:

> Having risen in the morning on the first day of the week, he appeared first to Mary of Magdala from whom he had cast out seven devils. She then went to those who had been his companions, and who were mourning and in tears, and told them. But they did not believe her when they heard her say that he was alive and that she had seen him.
>
> After this, he showed himself under another form to two of them as they were on their way into the country. These went back and told the others, who did not believe them either.
>
> Lastly, he showed himself to the eleven themselves while they were at table. And he said to them, "Go out to the whole world; proclaim the gospel to all creation. Whoever believes and is baptized will be

saved.... These are the signs that will be associated with believers: in my name they will cast out devils; they will have the gift of tongues; they will pick up snakes in their hands and be unharmed should they drink deadly poison; they will lay their hands on the sick who will recover."

Mark 16:9-18

The Church Spends Thirteen Weeks a Year Contemplating This

The resurrection of the Lord is revealed to the apostles and those who were with them while they were "at table." In the context of a meal Jesus appeared and showed himself as the one who has power over death. This is a powerful mystery. It is such a powerful mystery that the church spends six weeks in preparation each year to contemplate the meaning and riches of the paschal mystery, the passion, the death, and the resurrection of Jesus. This experience is called the season of Lent. The church then spends seven weeks contemplating the resurrection itself.

What Are You Going To Do for Lent?

What Jesus revealed "at table" demands time and prayer and process to come to grips with. We do this. We invest a great deal of time contemplating this mysterious grace each year. We call the time we spend preparing to plumb the richness of this event "Lent." Six weeks each year! This Is Impressive! I'd like to reflect on this phenomenon of Lent as a way to bring out the richness of what Jesus is sharing with those present with him "at table." Our common experience of Lent begins with an Ash Wednesday greeting of: "What are you going to do for Lent?" What emerges as a "gut reaction" from our collective uncon-sciousness of years and years of Catholic tradition may go something like this: "I'm going to give up candy" or "I'm going to give up alcohol" or "I'm going to go on a diet."

There can be another response to this season of Lent that deserves to be brought to light. Some will ask the question, "What do you, Lord, want me to do for Lent?" Obviously, this question is going to take some listening time on the part of the asker. It may take three days. It may take a week. It may take the first ten days of Lent before this question is answered by the Lord in prayer. This process encompasses other questions quite naturally as it proceeds and takes root in a person. "What are the people around me saying to me about me?" "What is life saying to me about me right now?" Putting these questions into the soup pot on the stove to simmer for some time in prayer as Lent begins usually results in a rich flavorful answer to the question. "What should I do for Lent?" This is one "job" that this season of Lent presents to us to do.

Another dynamic that presents itself during this time is to contemplate what Jesus is doing in the scriptures given us by the church's liturgy. The task is to keep our eyes on Jesus. This flows into the experience we have come to call "Holy Week," the church's liturgical proclamation of the passion, death, and resurrection of Jesus, the paschal triduum.

It is not as though we don't know what is going to happen during Holy Week. We have heard the story many, many times. There are no surprises. We know that Jesus will be betrayed in the heart of Judas on Spy Wednesday, that Jesus will celebrate the Passover with his disciples on Holy Thursday night, that Jesus will endure a trial, scourging, crucifixion, and death on Good Friday, that Holy Saturday will be a very vacant day, and that on that evening and on Easter Sunday we will commemorate the resurrection of Jesus. We know this.

To Give Jesus Applause

So what is the meaning of the sacred triduum, Holy Week, here for us? I think it is to celebrate what God has done for us in the suffering, passion, death, and resurrection of Jesus. It is for us to give Jesus praise, honor, glory, and applause for what he has done for us in that it was fine for him to suffer his passion, death, and resurrection for us. We were worth it to him. The paschal triduum, Holy Week, is a celebration of this.

As we give God glory and honor and praise and thanksgiving, we praise and applaud God in our hearts (the word *applaud* itself comes from the Latin word *laud* which means *praise*). As this continues throughout Holy Week, what begins to re-emerge as we give Jesus glory for carrying the cross for us is our own life—what we're called "to do" during Lent. We receive the grace of God revealing to us the truth of the glory of the cross of Christ. Here we begin to understand that Jesus "must suffer and die so as to enter into his glory" (Luke 24:26). The cross now blooms into a flower. We see the presence of Jesus Christ carrying his cross and the presence of Jesus on the cross of Calvary as glory, not as suffering. This is the grace of the paschal mystery. We glorify Christ on the cross. We celebrate the crucifixion of Christ. We give Jesus thanks and praise and honor for carrying his cross.

Our Cross Blooms into a Flower

As we give thanks and praise, the grace deepens. As we give Jesus glory, we experience Jesus turning to us and giving us glory for carrying our cross. As we give Jesus thanks we experience Jesus thanking us for carrying our cross. As this happens we experience our cross as the same cross that Jesus carries. Our cross is glorified. Our cross blooms and becomes a flower. We are glorified. Our cross, the one that we wish we did not have, is our glory—our cross, the one that we think that if we didn't have it all would be well, and we'd be home free inasmuch as our life would be what we always wanted. This cross is our glory. Our cross, the one that turns us inside out, is our glory. Not the cross that someone else has, and not the one that someone else has to carry, but the cross that only I have to carry—this is my glory.

The faces and dynamics that only I know of are on that cross. This is the cross that I am talking about. It is this cross that is glorified. It is this cross that is my glory. It is for my carrying of this cross that Jesus is glorifying and applauding me.

This is the resurrection!

To be able to turn to my cross with passionate love and carry it with joy is the grace of the resurrection!

There is only one person in all of existence that has the power to effect this capability in a human person. There is only one person who has the love to bring such a change about. It is Jesus! It is the power and the love of the resurrection of Jesus Christ. This is a huge gift! Most human beings spend their lives anesthetizing and running away from this reality within them. It is only in Christ that we can have the peace and the freedom to integrate and reconcile the reality of the cross in our lives. This is the grace of the passion, death, and resurrection of Jesus.

The grace of the resurrection of Jesus deepens as the risen Christ gifts the apostles here "at table" with the preaching of the gospel.

Go out to the whole world; proclaim the gospel to all creation.

Mark 16:15

A Sense of Being Sent by God Brings Freedom

This gift is one that effects what it proclaims. The very proclamation of the gospel has power. It is the power to change hearts into itself. It is a unique gift in that the preaching of the word of God by an apostle holds within it an implicit sense that one is sent by another and that one is a messenger of another. It is that one is to deliver what another would have one say. It is not the "word of an apostle" that the apostle is to preach but the "word of God." It is this sense that apostles have that they are sent by God that brings freedom. It is this sense that the "word" they speak is not their own but that their inspiration is that of the Holy Spirit of the risen Jesus that brings freedom and peace.

While They Were Eating at Table

This freedom and peace in the apostle is deepened by the injunction to preach the "word" to all creation. There is to be no one who is excluded from hearing the gospel. There is to be no obstacle worth attending to in this. One's past, race, sex, financial capability, educational level, career, health, age, talent, and maturity make no difference. The desire of God that all know the risen Jesus through the preaching of the gospel, the life, death and resurrection of Jesus, is clear by this command given while they were eating "at table."

Jesus tells of the signs that will accompany the preaching of the gospel that will validate the authenticity and origin of the "word." The most powerful of the signs is the simple belief engendered in the hearts and minds of the listeners that, "Yes, Jesus is Lord!"

The gift of knowing that Jesus of Nazareth is God of all life is beyond words. The gift of finding the meaning of our entire existence in Christ is awe-inspiring. When we think of the searching that human beings go through for this sense of meaning and the human energy involved in such a search, we get some sense of the value of this gift. The time and amassing of human resources in such an effort gives us some way to measure the importance of this gift.

As we contemplate this scene of the risen Christ at table sharing this gift, we again are brought to an understanding of what the real food of companionship and conversation mean.

Are you not aware that we who were baptized into Christ Jesus were baptized into his death? Through baptism into his death we were buried with him, so that, just as Christ was raised from the dead by the glory of the Father, we too might live a new life. If we

have been united with him through likeness to his
death, so shall we be through a like resurrection.

Romans 6:3-5

Our ability to embrace with passionate love and joyful
welcome the cross that is uniquely our own to carry is indeed
new life. It is a new phenomenon within human consciousness.
It is grace. This is the grace of the resurrection. The ability to
seek out and look for the broken body of the Lord among ourselves—our own sisters and brothers who are suffering their
own crucifixion on their own cross today—is grace. This hunger
to seek out the suffering Christ is the grace of the resurrection.
The desire to want to stay with Jesus on the cross and not abandon him in the lives of our brothers and sisters is the grace of
the resurrection of Jesus. This is what we are baptized into: the
grace of the death and resurrection of Jesus. It is right that this
grace was given "at table" as it is real food for our being.

Are There Examples of This Grace?

Are there examples of this grace-filled reality of the risen
Lord taking hold of a human being's life around us? Is the risen
Jesus present today in the lives of human beings of our time? I'd
like to say with joy, "Yes!" I'd like to share with you a personal
example, if I may.

I believe Mother Teresa of Calcutta is such an example. My
life began to become interwoven with hers some ten years ago,
when I went to Calcutta and gave talks on prayer to Mother
Teresa, the novice Missionaries of Charity, the professed sisters,
and the tertians, all of whom were of the congregation that
Mother Teresa founded. Giving a talk on prayer to Mother Teresa
was a bit intimidating, but after three minutes my good Jesuit
background and training took over, and I proceeded in peace.

In the midst of the experience, I spent a good amount of
time working in Calicut, the Home for Dying Destitutes, the first
home that Mother founded there in Calcutta. I walked in with

Sister Luke, M.C., and simply began by standing in a line of Missionary of Charity Brothers in the men's portion of the Home. The Brothers were there in line with towels waiting to dry men who were being showered in an adjoining room. As the men came around the corner from the shower room, they were dried by the next person in the line. This proceeded until I was the first person in line waiting for the next man to come around the corner from his shower. As I stood there waiting, a man came slowly around the corner. As I saw him I felt a firm jab in my lower back from the person behind me and a voice from behind me saying, "Leprosy! Leprosy!" I realized instantly as I saw the man round the corner that he was an open sore from head to foot. The man coming around the corner facing me had leprosy. I froze. I stood there for what seemed like an eternity, and, realizing that this is what I came for, I simply embraced the man with my towel. I dried him, took him to his bed, and fed him. After I did that I got back in the line and, as my turn came around again, I stood intently at the doorway to the shower room wondering and waiting, as once again I felt as if time had stood still. My eye was drawn downward as around the corner came the scraping sound of a man dragging himself along the ground. The man had no legs and was moving himself as he was accustomed—by pulling and lifting his torso by stiffening his arms and propelling himself forward. I bent down and dried him. Then I picked him up in my arms and took him to his bed.

Again I found myself back in the line to dry people as they came out of their morning shower. This time as I waited I saw one of the help backing through the door toward me. He was carrying a young boy. He was assisted by another helper from the shower room. They lifted the young boy, leaving him at my feet. As I looked down I saw a boy of some fifteen years of age. The boy was catatonic—paralyzed in the fetal position with his knees fixed to his chin. I dried the boy. I picked him up with the assistance of others and brought him to his bed. As I tended this boy, I realized that whatever it was that had happened to him in the streets—whatever it was—it had caused such fear and stress as to produce this protective reaction.

Was This Real? How Could This Be?

As my work there progressed, and as the shock of seeing what I was seeing began to lift, I was able to become aware of something I was sensing. Most of these people were dying. They would die, and soon. They were in very bad shape. Yet as I became aware of a feeling in the room, the feeling was one of joy. It was strange, and I began to check myself to see if I really was feeling this or not. Was this real? How could this be? It was real. And it was there. It was in each of these devastated and dying people. I could see it in their eyes. They were happy. And they were dying!

As I began to notice this, I found myself watching the sisters, the Missionaries of Charity. The sisters were medical doctors and registered nurses. I watched them put in I.V.'s and dispense medication as it was necessary. As they would bend over, putting in and finishing an I.V., they would stay there. They would hover over the person. They would stay there and stay there hovering over the person until the person broke out in a big smile. When that happened they were finished. They had done what they had come to do. They had loved that person.

They did not leave that person until that person had felt their love, until the person they were with felt loved, and until that individual had felt wanted. When that person felt wanted, felt loved, felt their love, they would move on to someone else.

"You Phonies!"

I began to understand and see where the joy in the room was coming from. These people, although they were dying, felt loved. These people, although they were dying, felt happiness. I'm sure many of the individuals there were feeling loved for the first time in their lives. I looked at the sisters, and I said to myself, "You phonies. You are using medicine to love these people. You are using nursing as an excuse to love these people, to make them feel your love, and to make them feel wanted."

This experience changed my life. Seeing what was before me implanted questions within me that will never go away: Are the people around me feeling my love? Are the people in my life feeling wanted by me? Are all of those around me in community, fellow workers, and friends getting the message that I love them? Are they feeling from me that they are wanted? The question was devastatingly challenging. I.V.'s are not enough! Service is not enough! Doing good works is not enough! Are those I'm serving feeling my love? Are they feeling wanted and valued by me during the activity I am engaged in with them? This question burned within me. Upon reflection it echoed the words of St. Paul in the first letter to the Corinthians:

> Set your mind on the higher gifts. And now I am going to put before you the best way of all. Though I command languages both human and angelic—if I speak without love, I am no more than a gong booming or a cymbal clashing. And though I have the power of prophecy, to penetrate all mysteries and knowledge, and though I have all the faith necessary to move mountains—if I am without love, I am nothing. Though I should give away to the poor all that I possess, and even give up my body to be burned—if I am without love, it will do me no good whatever.
>
> 1 Corinthians 13:1-3

This is an example of the resurrection of Jesus. This is the risen Jesus winning my heart with love.

The Feeling of Being Unwanted

Since I was giving talks on prayer to Mother Teresa and her novices, tertians, and professed sisters there at the Mother House and Tertian House in Calcutta, I had many opportunities to speak with Mother Teresa. In one of our early conversations, I was speaking with her about my work here in the United States.

I was telling her of the Jesuit Institute for Family Life. I was sharing with her our work of marriage counseling, family therapy, and individual counseling. She repeated to me words that she had spoken in her Nobel Peace Prize-winning speech in Oslo: "You know, I can go downstairs and out into the street and give a bowl of rice to someone lying there. That person will light up and thank me. You know, your job is harder than mine. Your job is harder. The poverty you work with is deeper." My reflections there and since then have led me to see that she is right. The depth of the feeling of being unwanted in the western world is in the men and women, children and adolescents we deal with in California in family therapy. It is covered over by wealth and technological conveniences and activities, but it is deeply there. A bowl of rice given can make someone light up and, indeed, there is a reward there for the giver. The reward of a smile is often long in coming to someone who feels unwanted in his or her family.

Real Food for Our Person

It is this love, God's love, that is embodied in Mother Teresa. It is this love that her sisters loved with in the Home for Dying Destitutes. It is this love, the love of God for us, that is the subject of this work. It is this love I wish to love with in my life. It is this love that I hope to image and show forth. And it is this love that I hope people feel in my presence. It is the fact that God loves every human being passionately that is the reality I wish to celebrate and give in my life and in this work. This love of God is real food for our person.

As I have stated, this experience changed my life. In Christ, Mother Teresa of Calcutta was real food for me. She showed forth the love of Jesus as totally as possible. In our conversations she made it clear that this gift was sustained from the eucharistic liturgy and from their daily hour of adoration before the eucharist. She expressed her experience in the words of John Henry Newman:

Dear Lord, help me to spread your fragrance everywhere I go. Flood my soul with your spirit and life.

Penetrate and possess my whole being so utterly that all my life may only be a radiance of you. Shine through me, and be so in me that every soul I come in contact with may feel your presence in my soul. Let them look up and see no longer me but only you, O Lord! Stay with me, and then I shall begin to shine as you shine, so to shine as to be a light to others. The light, O Lord, will be all from you; none of it will be mine; it will be you shining on others through me.

Let me thus praise you in the way you love best, by shining on those around me.

Let me preach you without preaching, not by words but by my example, by the catching force, the sympathetic influence of what I do, the evident fullness of the love my heart bears to you. Amen.

This is the kind of attitude that is enlivened in us as we watch Jesus love everyone at the communion rite of the eucharist.

This is what happens to Mother Teresa at the eucharist of Jesus today. Mother Teresa receives her call and her strength of love from the real food of the eucharist. What a gift to receive! The eucharist of Jesus is alive today as real food for us to feast on. Here is our source of nourishment. It happened to those present in the cenacle room long ago from the hand of Jesus himself. It happens to Mother Teresa now as Christ gives the love of God again. It is given to us today! We have Jesus Christ again today doing the same thing. Again and again at the eucharist he gives himself to everyone loving everyone with this love and calling us to do the same. He gives us the love of God to love with. It is the same God, the same gift, and the same love. It is real food. This is the resurrection.

QUESTIONS FOR PERSONAL AND COMMUNITY REFLECTION AND DISCUSSION

1. Do you do penance?

2. What do you do?

3. How do you come to know what penance to do? What is that experience like for you?

4. Share this in your group.

5. What is your experience of "Lent"?

6. Do you celebrate the passion and death of Jesus?

7. Do you experience the passion, death, and resurrection of Jesus as one event?

8. Do you praise Christ and give Jesus thanks for carrying his cross?

9. Have you experienced Jesus thanking you for the cross you carry?

10. Are you in love with the cross you have to carry?

11. What does the resurrection of Christ mean to you?

12. Do you see the suffering Christ in the suffering of those around you? Are you moved to comfort him?

13. Share these reactions with Jesus in your contemplation.

14. Share with your group your reactions to these questions.

Chapter Ten

The Breaking of the Bread: Emmaus

The exact biblical site of Emmaus is a point of dispute among contemporary scripture archaeologists. The general location is not. The consensus seems to be that Emmaus was somewhere north and west of Jerusalem, and, according to scripture, about "seven miles from Jerusalem." The terrain in this area is one of undulating hills, some moderately deep broad valleys beginning to extend their way toward the Mediterranean Sea. Here there is natural grassy cover which easily supports grazing. Walking in this direction from Jerusalem is not difficult. If we allow ourselves to contemplate this scene and place ourselves with these two disciples of Jesus we can get a flavor of the meaning of the event.

That very same day, two of them were on their way to a village called Emmaus seven miles from Jerusalem, and they were talking together about all that had happened. Now as they talked this over, Jesus himself came up and walked by their side; but something prevented them from recognizing him. He said to them, "What matters are you discussing as you walk along?" They stopped short, their faces downcast.

Then one of them, called Cleopas, answered him, "You must be the only person staying in Jerusalem who does not know the things that have been hap-

pening there these last few days." "What things?" he
asked. "All about Jesus of Nazareth," they answered,
"who proved he was a great prophet by the things he
said and did in the sight of God and of the whole
people; and how our chief priests and our leaders
handed him over to be sentenced to death, and had
him crucified. Our own hope had been that he would
be the one to set Israel free. And this is not all: two
whole days have gone by since it all happened; and
some women from our group have astounded us;
they went to the tomb in the early morning, and
when they did not find the body, they came back to
tell us they had seen a vision of angels who declared
he was alive. Some of our friends went to the tomb
and found everything exactly as the women had
reported, but of him they saw nothing."

Then he said to them, "You foolish men! So slow to
believe the full message of the prophets! Was it not
ordained that the Christ should suffer and so enter
into his glory?" Then, starting with Moses and going
through all the prophets, he explained to them the
passages throughout the scriptures that were about
himself.

When they drew near to the village to which they
were going, he made as if to go on; but they pressed
him to stay with them. Now while he was with them
at table, he took the bread and said the blessing; then
he broke it and handed it to them. And their eyes
were opened and they recognized him; but he had
vanished from their sight. Then they said to each
other, "Did not our hearts burn within us as he talked
to us on the road and explained the scriptures to us?"

They set out that instant and returned to Jerusalem.
There they found the eleven assembled together with

their companions, who said to them, "Yes, it is true. The Lord has risen and has appeared to Simon." Then they told their story of what had happened on the road and how they had recognized him at the breaking of bread.

Luke 24:13-35

To these two disciples all of the words Jesus spoke during his lifetime and all of the actions, miracles, and events of Jesus' life must have blurred as the experience of his crucifixion burned itself into their consciousness. We know how much time grieving takes. We know that part of the grieving process is remembering the experience of the death of a loved one. We know how important the need is at this time to share these memories with someone who is close to us. All of these elements are natural components of the human experience of loss and sorrow.

These two disciples were attempting to deal with the daze they were in and the pain they were experiencing with the loss of the one that they had put their hopes in for so long. They were in shock, and they seem to have been dealing with this in two significant ways. They were leaving the scene of their pain, Jerusalem, and they were talking about what they had experienced there. It was into this grief that Jesus immersed himself. We know how the conversation proceeded. We know that Jesus engaged the disciples as if he did not know what was going on. We know how he began to explain the scriptures to them concerning himself. The power of this encounter deepens as Jesus offers to move on when the disciples want to stop for an evening meal and lodging. They ask Jesus to stay with them. Jesus says that he will.

The Ability To Recognize Jesus Is a Gift

It is here that the drama of this encounter comes to its denouement. In the meal that they shared together Jesus took bread, blessed it, thanked God for the bread, and gave it to his disciples (Luke 24:30). As he did this, "their eyes were opened and they recognized him" (Luke 24:31). They recognized him in the breaking of the bread. Did these disciples have the power to recognize Jesus? The answer is "No, they did not!" Had they recognized Jesus during the long walk and discourse? No, they had not! The recognizing of Jesus was a grace. This was a grace from the hand of God. The ability to recognize Jesus was a gift from God. This experience of Jesus is a gift for our own contemplation as a source of great strength for our lives. Jesus gave the gift of recognizing who he was to these disciples as he broke the bread and shared it with them.

Jesus does the same today. Jesus gave these disciples the gift of recognizing who he was as he broke the bread and passed out his body and blood to eat as real food for their lives. His body was broken on the cross and his blood was poured out on the cross to give us this life. This sharing of his body and blood with these disciples presented them with the event of Jesus freely giving over his life for us in his passion, his crucifixion, his death, and his resurrection, the paschal mystery.

A Way That We Are Made Holy

This is "the way" Jesus has given us everlasting life. This gift is life forever. This is a gift of enormous importance for us. This is the greatest gift of our lives. This action comes from the imagination of God. It is a sacrament. It is an action, a happening among people, an event. It is social. The word "sacrament" comes from the Latin word *sacra*, which means holy, and the Latin word *mentum*—a means by which something is made holy. So, a definition of the word "sacrament" would be: a sacrament is a social event created by the imagination of God to make us holy. A sacrament is a gift of grace.

Jesus was present at a social event, a meal, in the inn at Emmaus. This action opened the eyes of the disciples to recognize Jesus. This grace present in this particular action is not a fluke. It is not a random occurrence. The grace present in this meal action of breaking the bread and pouring out the wine is purposeful on the part of God. The meal action contains and enshrines the dynamic power of God to change lives. In the imagination of God this meal action of breaking the bread and pouring out the wine is the breaking of the body of Christ and the pouring out of the blood of Christ—real food for us, real food for our lives, the real food of eternal life. It is in this action of the meal, the breaking of the bread and the pouring out of the wine, that grace was given to see Jesus. This happened at table during the meal at Emmaus. This same action happens in the eucharist of Jesus today.

Feast Your Eyes

In the eucharistic liturgy at the fraction rite and the communion rite we have the breaking of the bread, the pouring out of the wine, and the sharing of the body and blood of Christ with everyone who has celebrated this sacrament. It is a sight to see, to feast one's eyes on the actions taking place. This "recognizing him" is the same action which took place in the inn at Emmaus. The same grace is offered to us as we watch this action at the eucharist today. "They recognized him." This "recognizing him" is offered to us today if we keep our eyes open at the eucharist and see the eucharistic bread and wine, the body and blood of Christ, broken and shared with those coming up the communion line. Look at what is going on. Look at all the people coming up to communion. With our eyes open we can see Jesus giving over his very self to everyone. He gives himself to those we like, those we don't like, the rich, the poor, men, women, old people, children, the sick, the blind, the lame, blacks, Hispanics, orientals, whites, foreigners, heterosexuals, homosexuals, students, teachers, alcoholics, drug addicts— everyone, and even to me! This is who Jesus is. He invites all to his table to enjoy a meal with him. At this meal he gives himself over in love totally to everyone present. This is love. This is real food to see Christ in action. This is real food to see Christ giving himself lovingly to everyone.

If we see this, can we not be called and impelled to do the same? As we see Jesus' attitude toward people we know coming up to receive the person of Jesus, the body and blood of Christ, are we not drawn to have the same attitude as Jesus toward them? Are we not attracted to the freedom of loving with that same love of Jesus? Are we not empowered by what we see here to have the attitude Jesus has toward those we know who are coming up the communion line to receive the presence of God? This is real food. To be nurtured by what we see here is real food. This is why Jesus came: to feed us, to feed us on who he is, to feed us on who God is, and to feed us on the image and the actions of God. Jesus' gift is to show us God, and to have us feast our eyes on who God is. Here we have such a feast. Here we have such a sight each day at the eucharist.

Private Prayer and Public Prayer

The experience of seeing Jesus love everyone at the eucharist calls up for us the familiar distinction between private prayer and public prayer that has been given us down through the history of the church. Private prayer has always been encouraged. It has its own rules and its own rewards, as scripture has it:

> Go into your private room, and when you have shut the door, pray to your Father who is in that secret place, and your Father who sees all that is done in secret will reward you.
>
> Matthew 6:6

Public prayer is different. It is prayer done in public. It is prayer with other people present. The eucharist is public prayer. It is prayer prayed together with others. Every sacrament is public prayer. This type of prayer has its own rules and its own rewards as does private prayer. The rules and the rewards are different. The modality of grace in public prayer comes through the actions of the experience. The grace of God comes to us as we see and participate in the sacramental liturgical actions. So keeping our eyes open is a must. Watching the breaking of the bread, the pouring out of the wine, and the passing out of the body and blood of Christ is essential to receiving the grace meant for us. "Seeing is believing," as they say. Can you imagine the disciples at Emmaus keeping their eyes closed at the meal with Jesus and receiving the grace they did? It was precisely because they had their eyes open and their ears open at the meal with Jesus that they were nourished. They recognized Jesus.

Keep Your Eyes Open

It is the same for us today at the eucharist of Jesus. There is more real food for us at the eucharist of Jesus than his body and blood. There is the real food of watching Jesus move among the crowd and give himself to each person. Here is the power of the eucharist: to watch Jesus love people. Here is real food: to see Jesus' attitude toward my brothers and sisters. Real food is the love of God. The eucharist is Jesus presenting us as a gift to God, praying for us, and pleading for us before our Father. The eucharist is Jesus giving himself to everyone. We see this by keeping our eyes open at mass and in our watching what is going on. In our responding, in our participating, and in our public action, we are caught up in the grace God means us to have. We recognize Jesus. Recognizing Jesus is real food.

This is what we have to feast our eyes on during each eucharistic liturgy we attend. This is the real food given to us to eat in the communion rite of each eucharistic liturgy we attend. Watch Jesus break the bread and hand it out to everyone. This is real food. This is the grace of the sacrament of the eucharist given to make us holy.

QUESTIONS FOR PERSONAL AND COMMUNITY
REFLECTION AND DISCUSSION

1. Are you able to relate to the grieving process that the disciples of Jesus were experiencing as they traveled to Emmaus?

2. Are you able to welcome your own experiences of grief and loss?

3. How do you share with another person the experiences involved in your grief?

4. Are you able to recognize the reality of Jesus living out his life in the lives of your brothers and sisters?

5. What is your experience of the breaking of the bread and the pouring out of the wine at the fraction rite of the eucharistic liturgy?

6. Share your experience with your group.

7. What does the notion of sacrament mean to you?

8. Do you experience a sacrament as public prayer or private prayer?

9. How are the community actions at the eucharistic liturgy filled with God's loving grace and presence for you?

10. Share your response among the members of your group.

11. How does a sacrament make you "holy"?

12. Keep your eyes open watching the communion line as the handing out of the body and blood of Christ occurs in the next eucharistic liturgy you attend.

13. What is your experience of this liturgical action?

14. Is the eucharistic liturgy a feast for your eyes?

15. Share your experience in your community of believers.

Chapter Eleven

The Heavenly Banquet:
Surprise!

And I tell you many will come from east and west
and sit down with Abraham and Isaac and Jacob at
the feast in the kingdom of heaven.

Matthew 8:11

Jesus in this verse reveals to us a view of our future life: a
feast together. The words of Jesus at the meal he had with his
apostles before he suffered his passion, death, and resurrection
speak of the real food of eternal life. This eternal life is the eating, the drinking, the meal, and the table companionship and
conversation: the banquet of eternal life with God.

You are the ones who have stood by me faithfully in
my trials; and now I confer a kingdom on you, just as
my Father conferred one on me: you will eat and
drink at my table in my kingdom.

Luke 22:29-30

The book of Revelation speaks of heaven, the experience of
everlasting life, in these words:

Blessed are those who are invited to the wedding
feast of the Lamb.

Revelation 19:9

When we dwell on these words of scripture and their

meaning, their impact can be felt by us. What is being presented to us here for our contemplation? And what does it mean?

First of all, it is clear that Jesus is saying that heaven, everlasting life, will be a banquet, a meal, a feast together with him forever. Secondly, it is clear that all are invited, and many will be there. This meal will last for all eternity.

What does this mean for us? This question can be contextualized in a way that can bring it to life: What does this mean for us now? Adding the word "now" brings the dimension of time into the question. Since we live in time and since the subject is about time—eternity—it seems appropriate to bring this into our consideration.

The Power That the Past Has Over Us

What does this mean for us now? If we look at ourselves and at our lives as human beings, we know that we have our past to deal with, the present moment, and our future. We live in a world of time. Anyone who has tried to deal with his or her own past knows the power that the past has over us. Attempting to become free from our past is a very difficult process, and such an attempt reveals the strength of our past experiences.

The Power of the Future

Contemporary psychologists tell us from their testing that, granted the power the past has over a human being, the future has more power. A simple example of this is the way we get up in the morning on Saturday versus the way we get up on Monday morning. We get up on Saturday with verve and energy. It is a "day off," a holiday. We get up on Monday morning slowly, with pain, with a certain heaviness. What is going on here? It is the power of the future! When we get up in the morning on Saturday our future is "two days off" or "two days of 'holidays,'" Saturday and Sunday, because we don't have to go to the office and punch a time clock to make money. In other words, we don't have to go to work for two days. This is our immediate future. This immediate future has a definite and powerful impact on us. We feel great! We feel light! We feel energetic! We feel like doing something, going somewhere, whistling, and the like. On the other hand, when we get out of bed on a Monday morning, we are facing an immediate future of five eight to twelve hour working days. We get out of bed slowly, to say the least. Why? What is going on here? Our immediate future is not a "holiday," but rather the "work world." Our future impacts us deeply. We don't feel all that energetic. We don't feel all that "light," and we don't feel exactly like whistling. We sort of grope for the coffee. The difference in our "moods" here directly depends on our future and shows how deeply our futures affect us. This simple example brings to light the latest findings of research on human behavior that human beings are more affected by their futures than by their pasts.

If this is true, and I believe that it is, then look at the gift that the Lord Jesus is giving us as he reveals to us our future. What riches Jesus is offering us as he reveals the future of our human life! If human life is more impacted by its future than by its past, what is the value for human consciousness of determining its future? The value is beyond words. Look at what Jesus is presenting to us. Jesus is revealing to us that our entire future life for eternity will be in sharing a meal with him.

Our Future Is Love

Throughout this consideration we have seen what this means. Sharing a meal with Jesus is more than eating food to nurture our bodies. Sharing a meal with Jesus is being in the company of Jesus. It is breaking bread with Jesus. It is companionship with Jesus. Sharing a meal with Jesus is being engaged in conversation with Jesus. Sharing a meal with Jesus is eating the body and drinking the blood of Christ, real food for our person. It is communion with Jesus. The gift that Jesus is sharing with us here is that eternal life for us is companionship, conversation, and communion with him. It is a gift of love. Our future forever is to be spent being in love with our God who loves us. Our future is to be spent being loved by our God and loving God. Our future is to be spent with our God who is love. Our future is love.

One way for us to comprehend the value of this gift of spelling out our future is to consider what we would be like without it. Can you imagine what it would be like reading the front page of the morning paper without knowing that your entire future life is to be spent with a God who loves you forever? Can you imagine what it would be like watching the one-hour local news on television every evening without knowing you will be spending forever being loved intimately by our personal God? I'm sure, if you are like me, and you spend any time with this possibility, that the only honest reaction would be depression. This depression would only validate the contemporary research in psychology that human beings are more motivated by the future than by the past. If we look at what is happening on the front page of the morning newspaper without knowing that our lives will be spent with a God who loves us forever, we are faced with a "now" experience that is very often painful.

When we look at the gift Jesus is giving us, the revelation of our own future as a banquet meal with him and our sisters and brothers in love forever, have we not seen this before? The revelation of this gift does not seem strange or unnatural. We have seen this before. We have seen Jesus eat with our sisters and brothers in his life with us. It is not strange that what Jesus longed to do with us here in our lives he would long to do forever with us.

Jesus spoke often of everlasting life, of how his reign was within us now, and of the interplay of our future life together with him and of our life now together. Jesus spoke often of eternal life being in us now.

Jesus' World Is One of Relationships

Jesus' speaking about eternal life is what makes him so attractive. Jesus' speaking of love is what makes him mesmerizing. Jesus is "the first-born of all creation" (Col 1:15) because of how he does things. Jesus is "the first-born of all creation" because he wins the human heart with love. This is why Jesus is "the first-born of all creation." The human heart is won by many things: by power, by money, by honors, by lust, and by willfulness. Jesus chooses not to win the human heart by any of these means. Jesus chooses only love. Jesus offers only love as his reign. Jesus' reign is a reign of relationship. Jesus' concern is a concern about relationship. Jesus' interest is in relationship. Jesus' reign is not of power or influence or money or worldly honor or riches or manipulative seduction. Jesus' world is one of relationship in love. This is what makes Jesus so attractive, and Jesus' followers are aslo attractive because of this way of life.

Is this strange? I don't think so. Jesus states that all of the law and the prophets can be summed up in this:

Love one another as I have loved you.

John 15:12

Jesus continually says that his way of love is who he is and what his reign is all about. This is what we have seen over and over again throughout his life. We have been given Jesus' life to contemplate, and we have been given this life of Jesus so that we will know who God is.

Look at All That Happened During Meals

Look at all that happened during the meals of Jesus. Look at the real food he gave: the conversation, the sharing of who he was, the sharing of his very self in word and in action. See the companionship he shared!

As we look back over the people Jesus chose to celebrate a meal with in Cana of Galilee, we see simple country men and women. We see Jesus' love for them in his valuing their presence and feelings. When we see Jesus share a meal with Levi, we see tax collectors whose ilk was rejected as scum. We see Jesus' love extending itself seeking these people out. When we remember Tabgha and the feeding of the five thousand we look at them. We look at Jesus. We see the people lost and wandering after Jesus as sheep looking for a shepherd. We see the love of Jesus for them, for the sick, for the hungry among them. Jesus' love goes out to all of them. Jesus feeds them all.

Jesus' eating a meal with the scribes and Pharisees presents itself as an image here. Jesus' love goes out to his enemies: to those who were jealous of him and who wanted him removed from their world. Jesus reaches out in love to them.

Jesus loves Zacchaeus and the rich. He shares a meal with the rich and offers them the real food of his love to them. The desire of Jesus for us is beginning to show itself. The passion of the love of Jesus for us is beginning to become irrational.

Jesus' love of women emerges as he shares himself with the woman who was a sinner at the home of the Pharisee. Jesus expresses his unabashed love of this woman by sharing his love for her as food for all of those present. The foolishness of the love of God introduces itself.

The real food of the love Jesus shows the twelve Galilean apostles at the last meal he had with them opens for us just how deeply his passion is. He shares his call and image of service in the washing of the feet. He shares his command that we must love one another as he has loved us. He gives the food of seeking the will of his Father. He shares his own body and blood with these nobodies. The illogic of his love establishes itself as the real food of our lives.

With the two disciples at Emmaus Jesus shares a meal and breaks into human consciousness his eucharistic love and presence for all people for all time. They recognized Jesus as he broke the bread. The love of God has incarnated itself in the breaking of the bread at our daily celebration of the eucharist of

Jesus for all people for all time. This is the reaching out of God to those he loves: all people of all time. God loves the poor, the rich, the ignorant, the educated, sinners, holy men and women, mediocre men and women, children, and the old. This is who God is. Surprise!

They Keep Coming Up the Communion Line

It is a surprise to see who God is. It is a constant surprise. As we keep our eyes open at the breaking of the bread and the communion rite of the eucharist of Jesus today and watch Jesus' love, we are surprised whom he loves. As we keep our eyes open at the eucharistic celebration and watch who comes up the communion line and whom Jesus gives himself completely to, it is a surprise whom God loves. God loves those in the community we think shouldn't be there. God loves those in the community whose personal lives we are privy to and, because of that, who we know are unworthy. God loves those in the community whose problems are radically affecting the smooth functioning of the parish. God loves those in the community with whom we disagree. God loves those in the community whose theology is questionable. God loves those in the community who don't know how to raise their children. They keep coming up the communion line. Jesus gives himself totally to them.

Christ gives himself to those who are unreliable, to those who are irresponsible, to those whose personal history has rendered them emotionally crippled for life, and to those who are incapable of intimacy. Jesus gives himself to those who have deep-seated repressed anger, to those who we know need ten years of group therapy yet will not hear of it, and to compulsive talkers. Christ loves those who want to know everything about you and who spread it over the telephone instantly and those who are preoccupied with gaining control of the religious education program of the parish. Christ loves those who think the celebrant of the eucharist is incompetent. The list is endless. The communion line is endless. Look at it! See them! See whom Jesus has chosen to give himself totally to! Surprise! Surprise!

How Do You Tell Real Food?

What do you think? Is there a call to do the same? Is there a call to be like Jesus? Is there a call for us to share ourselves in conversation? Do we share the real food of who we are with others at our meals? Do we share the real food of companionship with others at mealtime? Is our life fed with this real food? Or is everything in our lives and loves "fast food"? Are we starving for real food: the real food of unconditional love of everyone? This love of Jesus for everyone is the real food for our being, our souls, our personhood, and our existence.

This is real food. How do you tell? How do you tell real food from junk food? By the energy it gives! We are able to tell the real from the unreal by its effect on us. We somehow have within us a sense of estimation that roams around what we are perceiving and experiencing, searching out whether what is out there will satisfy us or not. Somehow in our guts and in our hearts and in our selves we know. We can tell the real from the unreal. We know real food from junk food by the strength it gives us, from the intensity and vigor we feel, from the vitality and animation it gives. Real food nourishes us. It provides verve and deep stamina.

Watching Jesus Love Is Real Food

Watching Jesus love us is real food. Watching Jesus love us at his eucharist is real food for us. Watching Jesus satisfies us and gives us energy. It confers vitality and strength. Watching Jesus love people is real food as it nourishes us with love and calls us irresistibly into Jesus' own love of everyone. This is the energy this real food imparts: a vocation to love as Jesus loves.

So this real food satisfies because it invites us to be changed into what we are seeing. Watching Jesus love all people at each eucharist by giving his total self to everyone who comes up the communion line changes us into being Jesus' own presence in the world. This is what vitalizes us. This is the real food for human life: to be the presence of God to all of our sisters and brothers. This is what we hunger for. And this real food of watching Jesus love people is the only food that will satisfy us and make us what we have always wanted to be.

"We are what we eat" is a famous quote. We also are what we watch. We are turned into what we see. If our eyes are on Jesus loving everyone at each eucharist we go to, we will be changed into what we are looking at. This love of Jesus that we see during communion at each eucharist has within it the power to change us. We can only "love one another as I (Jesus) have loved you" (John 15:12) by keeping our eyes on Jesus. It is in this way that we will be Jesus' hands, and arms, and eyes, and love in the world.

This is the real food that Jesus came to feed us, for he came that we "may have life and have it to the full" (John 10:10). It is the intention of our God that we be who God has created us to be. As St. Irenaeus put it in the second century, "the glory of God is a person fully alive." Our God is providing a meal of real food for us. We are invited.

We are given an invitation to feast on the real food of who Jesus is because the food God gives at the banquet of Jesus is the very self of Jesus to eat, Jesus to share with, and Jesus as companion. The food of God is a relationship. The real food of human life is relationship. The real food of our lives is relationship with God.

Surprise!

We are drawn into relationship—relationship with God, relationship with each other, and relationship with our very self. Our real food is relationship? Yes. This is what really feeds us? Yes. Where do we get this need, this orientation?

We, men and women, are made in the image and likeness of God. Is this true or untrue? We say it is true. We agree. We assent to this. This is implicit in all we say and do as Christians. If this is true, that we are made in the image and likeness of God, and if it is true that our food is relationship, this must say something about God. What could this say about God? If relationship is so important to us, relationship must be important to God. If we look closely, we can see that this is true.

Surprise!

We have a very unique God as far as the history of gods is concerned. We say that our God is three persons in one God, a Trinity. Within this mystery of one God we say that there are three distinct persons: the Father, Jesus, and the Holy Spirit. Our God is an "in relationship" God. the Father relating to Jesus the Son who is relating to the Holy Spirit who is relating to Jesus who is relating to the Father. Our God is three persons who are relating to each other. Our God is a relationship. We worship a relationship. Surprise!

Surprise!

This is where we get our fixation on relationship. We are created in the image and likeness of God, who is a relationship. This is where we get the hunger for relationship. We are created in the image and likeness of God, who is a relationship. This is where we get the food we need to be who we have always wanted to be. We receive this in and from our God who is a relationship. God allows us to feed upon who God is: the Father relating to Jesus, Jesus relating to the Father and the Holy Spirit, and the Holy Spirit relating to Jesus and the Father.

This relational love and action of each person of the Trinity, our God, is what goes to make up the very meaning of human life. It is the ground of human history. The Father sending Jesus into the world was an act of love for us from our God. The Holy Spirit acting in the hearts of women and men attracting them to Jesus is a loving act for us from God. Jesus drawing us and bringing us to his Father is an act of love of us from our God. This is our God loving. This is human life being caught up in how each person of our God loves and relates to each other person of the Trinity. This is salvation history.

Like a New Baby at a Family Picnic

Our own experience of relating to our God is very much like being a new baby in the family. As the whole extended family gathers for a picnic, the new baby in the family gets welcomed by being passed from one family member to another during the picnic. Each member of the family tweaks the cheek of the new baby, holds the new baby up in the air, makes the new baby smile, and then passes the new baby on to the next person.

This is what it is like to relate to our God, a Trinity, three persons. We are passed from one person of our God to another like a new baby at a family picnic. The joy of our God is to bring us into their relationship.

We have this relating of our God in the eucharistic liturgy. In the liturgy of the word, we are drawn to Jesus by the power of the Holy Spirit as we hear the word of God read and preached. In the eucharistic prayer, Jesus brings us as his own to the Father as a gift and prays for us. In the communion rite, the breaking of the bread and the passing out of the body and blood of Christ, Jesus feeds each human person with his love. Here we are caught up in the relating of our God, the Trinity. We are made one with God in the loving action and grace of the love of the Father for Jesus, and the love of Jesus for the Holy Spirit, and the love of the Holy Spirit for Jesus. This is what Jesus prayed for at his supper meal with his apostles:

> May they all be one
> just as, Father, you are in me and I am in you,
> so that they also may be in us
> so that the world may believe it was you who sent me.
> I have given them the glory you gave to me.
> With me in them and you in me,
> may they be so perfected in unity

that the world will recognize that it was you who sent me and that you have loved them as you loved me.

John 17:21-23

This is the prayer of Jesus for us at the eucharistic liturgy.

Our food is to feast our eyes on our God. Our meal is to commune with our God. This is the banquet God offers us: real food. This is the banquet meal we are invited to attend forever. This is eternal life.

We are invited. Surprise!

QUESTIONS FOR PERSONAL AND COMMUNITY REFLECTION AND DISCUSSION

1. How are you affected by your past? What is your experience of being affected by your past?

2. How are you affected by your future? What is the effect of your future experiences on you? What does this feel like?

3. Are you more affected by your future than by your past?

4. Share your reaction with your group.

5. Spend time in prayer considering the value of knowing that your future is going to be one of love with a God who loves you passionately.

6. Share your prayer experience in your group.

7. How do you envision everlasting life?

8. How do you experience eternal life now? Is this real food for you? How do you experience this?

9. Share your experience with your group.

10. Is a relationship with God an experience of being fed with real food for you?

11. Are you fed real food by watching Jesus at each eucharist give his entire self to everyone who comes up the communion line?

12. Share your response in your group.

13. What is your experience of the Trinity?

14. What does the fact that our God is three persons mean to you?

15. What is your experience of being caught up in the relating of God to Jesus to the Holy Spirit?

16. Share your experience among your group members.

17. Are you surprised?

Bibliography, References, and Suggested Readings

Allen, Ronald B. *I Will Praise Him: Worship in the Psalms.* Nashville: Thomas Nelson Publisher, 1992.

Alonso-Schoekel, Luis, S.J. *Celebrating the Eucharist.* New York: Crossroad, 1989.

Bausch, W. *A New Look at the Sacraments.* Mystic: Twenty-Third Publications, 1983.

Benoit, P., R. Murphy, et al. *The Breaking of Bread (Concilium).* New York: The Seabury Press, 1961.

Bernardin, Joseph Cardinal. *Christ Lives in Me.* Cincinnati: St. Anthony Press, 1985.

Brown, Raymond E. *New Testament Essays.* New York: Paulist Press, 1965.

_____. *Responses to 101 Questions on the Bible.* New York: Paulist Press, 1990.

_____. *A Risen Christ in Eastertime.* Collegeville: Liturgical Press, 1990.

Brown, et al. *Peter in the New Testament.* New York: Paulist Press, 1973.

Burghardt, Walter. J., S.J. *Dare To Be Christ*. New York: Paulist Press, 1991.

Byrne, Brendan, S.J. *Inheriting the Earth. A Pauline Basis of a Spirituality for Our Time*. New York: Alba House, 1991.

Canale, Andrew. *Understanding the Human Jesus*. New York: Paulist Press, 1985.

Corbon, Jean. *The Wellspring of Worship*. New York: Paulist Press, 1988.

DeCaussade, Jean-Pierre. *The Sacrament of the Present Moment*. New York: Harper and Row, 1989.

de la Potterie, Ignace, S.J. *The Hour of Jesus. The Passion and Resurrection According to John*. New York: Alba House, 1990.

Fabing, Robert, S.J. *The Eucharist of Jesus*. Phoenix: North American Liturgy Resources, 1986.

_____. *Experiencing God in Daily Life*. Phoenix: North American Liturgy Resources, 1991.

Faricy, Robert, S.J. *The Lord's Dealing*. New York: Paulist Press, 1988.

Feider, Paul A. *The Sacraments: Encountering the Risen Lord*. Notre Dame: Ave Maria Press, 1986.

Fisher, Eugene (ed.). *The Jewish Roots of Christian Liturgy*. New York: Paulist Press, 1990.

Fitzpatrick, Joseph P., S.J. *Paul: Saint of the Inner City*. New York: Paulist Press, 1990.

Froehle, Virginia Ann, R.S.M. *Called into Her Presence: Praying with Feminine Images of God*. Notre Dame: Ave Maria Press, 1992.

Gelineau, Joseph. *The Liturgy Today and Tomorrow*. New York: Paulist Press, 1978.

Guardini, Romano. *Sacred Signs*. Wilmington: Michael Glazier, Inc., 1979.

Hassel, David J., S.J. *Radical Prayer*. New York: Paulist Press, 1984.

Healey, Charles J., S. J. *A New Song to the Lord*. New York: Alba House, 1991.

Hellwig, Monika. *The Eucharist and the Hunger of the World*. New York: Paulist Press, 1976.

_____. *The Meaning of the Sacraments*. Dayton: Pflaum, 1972.

Hunter, David G. *Preaching in the Patristic Age*. New York: Paulist Press, 1989.

The Jerusalem Bible. Garden City: Doubleday and Company, 1985.

Jones, Cheslyn, Geoffrey Wainwright, and Edward Yarnold, S.J., eds. *The Study of Liturgy*. England: Oxford University Press, 1978.

_____. *The Study of Spirituality*. England: Oxford University Press, 1986.

Jungmann, Josef A. *The Place of Christ in Liturgical Prayer*. Collegeville: The Liturgical Press , 1989.

Keating, Thomas. *Reawakenings*. New York: Crossroad, 1992.

Knopp, Robert. *Finding Jesus in the Gospels*. Notre Dame: Ave Maria Press, 1989.

Maloney, George A., S.J. *In Jesus We Trust*. Notre Dame: Ave Maria Press, 1990.

Martin, George. *Praying with Jesus*. Liguori: Liguori Publications, 1989.

Martini, Carlo M., S.J. *Ministers of the Gospel*. New York: Crossroad, 1989.

McBrien, Richard. *Ministry*. San Francisco: Harper and Row, 1988.

McGehee, Michael D. *God's Word Expressed in Human Words: The Bible's Literary Forms*. Collegeville: The Liturgical Press, 1991.

Moltmann-Wendel, Elisabeth. *The Women Around Jesus*. New York: Crossroad, 1982.

Neyrey, Jerome, S.J. *The Passion According to Luke*. New York: Paulist Press, 1985.

O'Collins, Gerald. *Jesus Risen*. New York: Paulist Press, 1987.

Osborne, Kenan, O.F.M. *Sacramental Theology*. New York: Paulist Press, 1988.

Pennington, M. Basil, O.C.S.O. *Call to the Center. The Gospel Invitation to Deeper Prayer*. New York: Doubleday, 1990.

Powers, Joseph M. *Eucharistic Theology*. New York: Herder and Herder, 1972.

Rahner, Karl, S.J. *Inspiration in the Bible*. New York: Herder and Herder, 1966.

_____. *The Church and the Sacraments*. New York: Herder and Herder, 1963.

Richter, Klemens. *The Meaning of Sacramental Symbols*. Collegeville: The Liturgical Press, 1990.

Rosage, David E. *Encounters with Jesus*. Ann Arbor: Servant Publications, 1987.

Schillebeeckx, Edward, O.P. *Revelation and Theology*. New York: Crossroad, 1984.

_____. *Christ: The Experience of Jesus as Lord*. New York: Crossroad, 1990.

Senior, Donald, S.P. *The Passion of Jesus in Luke*. Wilmington: Michael Glazier, 1989.

Sheldrake, Philip, S.J. *Images of Holiness*. Notre Dame: Ave Maria Press, 1988.

Swenson, Roger A. *Prayer and Remembrance*. Notre Dame: Ave Maria Press, 1989.

Underhill, Evelyn. *Worship*. New York: Crossroad, 1982.

Westerhoff, John H. *Living the Faith Community*. Minneapolis: Winston Press, 1985.